STREET CREDS

ZACH FORTIER

steeleshark
press

Cover design, interior book design
and eBook design
by Blue Harvest Creative
www.blueharvestcreative.com

STREET CREDS

Copyright © 2012, 2013 Zach Fortier

Published by
SteeleShark Press

ISBN-13: 978-0615849478
ISBN-10: 0615849474

Visit the author at:
Website: *www.curbchek.com*
Blog: *www.authorzachfortier.blogspot.com*
Facebook: *www.facebook.com/pages/StreetCreds/166796290069823*
Twitter: *www.twitter.com/zachfortier1*
Goodreads: *www.goodreads.com/author/show/5164780.Zach_Fortier*

THIS BOOK IS DEDICATED TO MY QUIET SON

SHALLEN DEMETRIUS LESTRICK
"DOUGHBOY"

BORN: MONDAY, SEPTEMBER 3, 1979
DIED: WEDNESDAY, OCTOBER 2, 2013

Preface

Street Creds is a look inside the world of street gangs and the cops that work them.

I worked the street for many years before I entered the Gang Task Force, joining it with the idea that I ***could*** rise to the level of violence of any banger I encountered—a really stupid idea.

I wanted to "earn back" the respect of the citizens for the police; I grew up in this city, and I worked its streets the best way I knew how, feeling that I had a firsthand understanding of what the citizens were experiencing.

The increasing frustration at gang crimes, drive bys, robberies, never feeling safe with your kids in your own neighborhood.

Once I was inside the task force, though, the reality was a rude awakening for me. The task force was poorly managed and staffed by detectives mostly out for themselves, and the internal politics made success incredibly difficult and almost impossible—almost, but not quite.

Witnessing bad cops, brutal crimes, and realizing the department had been compromised, the cost was much higher for me personally than I anticipated.

I left the unit two years later, severely broken, edgy, and dangerously damaged.

Street Creds is the story of how all that came to be.

Zach Fortier

STREET CREDS

"Earning or possessing a high level of respect on the street. A reputation gained by repeated experience on the street or in the penal system."

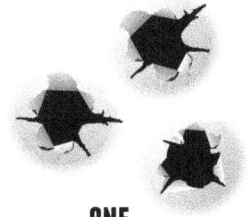

INITIATION RITES

MY FIRST WEEK ON THE Gang Task Force, I was attending a Gang Seminar in Dallas.

I was pretty excited to attend; I thought that we were going to meet a lot of experts from across the nation and hopefully get some new insight into how to make an impact on the gang problem.

But the reality was quite different; instead, we were surrounded by academics who were only concerned with studying philosophical, obscure theories about gang behavior.

There was no representation from anyone with actual practical expertise.

For example, one presenter felt that gang members joined the gang due to a lack of being able to play when they were younger. She felt that if gang members were allowed to "re-experience" childhood *(playing on swings, merry-go-rounds, and teeter-totters)*, they'd properly develop psychologically and no longer be interested the gang life.

This was typical of the bullshit that various researchers presented in an effort to validate their work.

I went from seminar to seminar, looking for anyone who had something valid and useful to teach me; I found very little.

Meanwhile, the crew that I went to the seminar with was only interested in playing hooky in the hotel rooms, sleeping and hitting the strip clubs at night; they could've cared less about trying to learn anything— but of course, they'd report back to the department that the seminar was well worth the expense and that they'd returned with valuable tools and insight.

I was transferred to the Gang Task Force to replace Detective Jim Smally, who had joined the task force about a year-and-a-half prior with some knowledge about gangs.

He knew a few gang members and was really excited that he might be able to make a difference.

One night after I was selected for the task force, Smally asked me, "Where do you think that the Gang Task Force needs to concentrate the majority of its efforts?"

He was eager to make an impact in an area that no one had addressed before, make his mark and carve out a new trail, so to speak.

I think he wanted to change the way the task force was perceived and have people in the department take it seriously.

I told him that I thought the previous group on the Gang Task Force had neglected the 18th Street gang and that they were a big problem that really needed to be addressed.

The previous guys working gangs had dismissed the 18th Street members as wannabes and saw them as no real threat.

What we were dealing with on the streets of St. Pauls was an offshoot of the original gang in L.A., where they are considered to be the largest and most active of transnational criminal gangs.

When I had expressed my disagreement with them regarding their position, I was ridiculed for it.

I told Smally about how I'd noticed that gang members were especially susceptible to praise and kindness, tempered with a hard edge.

I told him that this was the technique that I used to earn their trust, and I suggested he try it.

Jim took that suggestion and ran with it, and for the first year in gangs he did exceptionally well in the intelligence-gathering portion of the job.

He collected an amazing amount of information on 18th Street: who the members were, how the internal structure worked, and who the leaders were, and he even learned that there was more than one subset of 18th Street; he found out that there were at least two subsets represented in St. Pauls: West Side 18th Street and South Side 18th Street.

He also found out that they weren't always on friendly terms with each other, having different leadership and different goals.

He accomplished all of this in a really short period of time.

Surprisingly, though, his weakness was the same as the gang members—and they exploited it.

He was considered an outcast in the police department.

He and I had been on SWAT together, and he'd been forced to resign because he didn't fit in with the "in crowd" *(the Leeds, Divot, and Peabody crowd)*.

He was a former Marine, and they liked the bragging rights that gave the team, but they didn't like that he was an independent thinker who wouldn't blindly follow orders that didn't make sense.

When he went to gangs and started to befriend the gang members, they accepted him and actually liked him; as a result, he started to lose perspective and started hanging out with them off duty—even going to an 18th Street gang member's wedding.

He had his picture taken at the wedding and made the mistake of showing it to Mike Vetere, his partner in gangs.

Vetere had made a career out of making himself look good to the brass by being their snitch; he'd back channel information to them on what was going on in whatever unit he was associated with at the time.

He was instrumental in getting Dave Session and Rob Rinker removed from the task force, which he accomplished either by exaggerating things that they did with gang members or describing their activities to the brass in a way that was less than complimentary.

Meanwhile, he made himself out to be the sole person on the Gang Task Force that had a handle on the street and what was going on in the gangs.

He also frequently made things up and claimed to have information on cases that he never closed or made arrests on.

Whenever he was questioned about this, he'd claim that the other detectives had ruined his credibility on the street or had warned a witness that he was coming.

He played Jim Smally hard and had him believing that he could trust him and that they could work together, even stating to Jim that he finally had a partner in gangs who understood what needed to be done.

I warned Smally about Vetere, but he didn't listen.

He told me that he and Vetere had an understanding, a partnership, and that they were "in the fight together."

I wouldn't associate with Vetere, and I told Jim that, making it really clear that I wouldn't help him with Vetere in the conversation.

If he wanted my help, he'd have to come to me alone—or not at all.

He thought I was being paranoid *(I heard that a lot)*, and he told me that he and Vetere had hung out together off duty, had parties with each other's families and children, and that he trusted Vetere above anyone else in the department.

When Vetere saw the picture of Smally at the 18th Street wedding, he finally had the hard evidence he needed to take Smally off the task force—once again making himself look like the only one that the brass could trust to get things done.

He went straight to the brass and told them that "Smally had been compromised by the 18th Street gang" and that he needed to be removed from the task force.

He then showed them the picture of Smally at the wedding—and it took about three seconds for the brass to decide to remove him.

Smally finally came to me one night and told me, "You were right; Vetere has screwed me."

This was partially true; Smally had lost perspective as well.

He started out on the task force convicting gang members of the crimes that they were committing, but toward the end he was letting them slide, making cases drag on and on until the victims lost interest and covering for the gang members with whom he'd formed friendships.

It became so blatant that a deputy county attorney contacted the police department and complained that none of the cases being filed by the Gang Task Force were being won in court—and it wasn't because they weren't winnable; it was because the task force was incapable of turning in cases of conviction quality.

Vetere sidestepped this accusation by claiming that he'd done every-thing he could to make the cases conviction quality, but that Smally had been running interference and sabotaging his cases.

This did happen in detectives a lot.

Your fellow detective can be your worst enemy; it was a very competitive, dog-eat-dog environment, so it wasn't an outrageous claim.

Feeling betrayed again by the department, when he was told that he was being removed from gangs, Smally sabotaged the gang files.

He removed the pictures of gang members that he wanted protected, and he purged the gang lists as well; so, when I went in as his replacement, the gang lists were incomplete, the files were in shambles, and several hundred pictures of gang members were missing.

When I was selected for the task force, Vetere came to me and did the same thing that he'd done to everyone else in the unit: he claimed that he wanted to work together and collaborate on cases.

He praised me for my knowledge of gangs and the street and asked that I show him what I'd learned.

I made it very clear to him, though, that I worked alone.

I'd witnessed how he'd fucked over his partners—and I would *not* be his next victim.

I told him exactly that, using those exact words and letting him know that from that point on he'd be on his own.

I'd help him on other cases that he'd been given if he asked me to, but I wouldn't work with him in any other fashion—period.

This really pissed him off, but he ended up leaving the unit about three months later, along with his record of zero cases closed with an arrest and conviction of a gang member.

During my first week, while I was at the seminar in Dallas, the Sergeant came to me and said, "Zach! I have your first case. Councilman Young's house was shot at in a drive by, and it's all yours."

I didn't mind getting the case, but I thought that this was stupid.

I was in another state, at least a week away from being able to do anything meaningful on the case; meanwhile, there were other detectives on the task force who had stayed behind and hadn't attended the seminar.

They had the background experience and could've begun working on the case immediately. It just didn't make any sense.

Later, I found out that there had been a big battle over the case and no one wanted it, and if it wasn't solved there would be political fallout between the city council and the police department.

Councilman Young had never been a friend of the police department, and he'd complain nonstop until an arrest was made.

Giving me the case would make the task force look like it had done nothing to solve it for some time.

This was how it was managed: it was a group of people who didn't like working gang cases and didn't understand gang members—but all wanted the title of "Detective", the schedule, and the perks that came with the job.

So, I was stuck with a case of "give this one to the new guy."; no one else wanted it, and several flat out refused to work it.

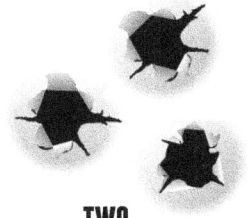

COUNCILMAN AT LARGE

I ARRIVED BACK AT THE department a week later, and during my first hour back the Lieutenant called me in and wanted to know what I'd done on the case.

I replied that I'd just gotten back from the seminar and that I hadn't even been in the building twenty minutes—what did he expect me to have done?

He told me not to make excuses, that he wanted results and expected an arrest by the week's end.

This was ridiculous; he'd let the case sit for a week-and-a-half already with absolutely nothing done on it—and NOW he wanted results.

I didn't want to end up like Smally, losing perspective, or like Vetere with no cases reaching conviction quality; yet, here I was faced with the culture of a task force set up for failure.

It made me realize that it wasn't as simple as becoming too close to the gangs or being accepted by the gang leaders.

With all the criticism that the Gang Task Force received in the department, I could understand that this wasn't hard to fall victim to.

Nothing was ever good enough; the more you accomplished in arrests, the more the other detectives hated you and were jealous of you—and the less you accomplished, the more you were seen as too soft and incompetent.

It was a no-win scenario.

So, I came in and decided to try to make a statement.

I'd be a friend to whoever worked with me, inside or outside the department, but I wouldn't compromise when it came to shooters.

I made that commitment for two years, doing whatever it took to get the shooters off the streets, then after two years I'd bounce. *(Two years was the most a "working" detective had survived in the Gang Task Force; after that, they'd been kicked out and discredited, having fallen from grace in the latest purge of the unit.)*

I made it a personal goal never to lose a case I made an arrest on; I had to get the conviction, not just the arrest.

If they were in a shooting or thought about doing a shooting, I had to make bangers realize that I'd be coming for them, arrest them, and convict them—no matter what.

As for the other detectives, they were either friend or foe, with no in-between—and there were very few friends.

I printed the case and read the facts.

Officer Dave Stils had written the original case.

He was a former military guy whom I disliked immensely; he had a very annoying habit of always finishing your sentences for you when he talked.

Additionally, regardless of the subject you talked about, he always knew more than you and had already done more than you could ever possibly do yourself.

He'd written a very basic case, having taken whatever Young had said at face value.

He'd collected evidence and obtained some witnesses' names, but he'd taken no pictures or statements.

Additionally, he'd shown no relationship between the suspects and the Young family; in other words, there was no apparent reason for the shooting.

It was reported as "random", but the Youngs knew who the suspect was and what car he drove.

There were a lot of unanswered questions, and after working on the case for about a week, here's what I found out:

First, the entire Young family had been heavily involved in gangs.

The sons and daughter were all members of the WSP *(West Side Pirus)*, which had been rolled into the SPVG *(St. Pauls Violent Gangsters)* under Jessie Afuvi's leadership.

Young tried to present himself as in touch with the streets, a "people's councilman" in touch with the needs of his area of representation; but, the reality was that he was the father of gang members, and on the weekends he drank beer and had barbeques with gang members in the park—not as a politician trying to keep in touch with his constituents, but as a friend and colleague.

The legitimate citizens didn't attend his parties and cookouts; they didn't like him or trust him.

His daughter had been dating a South Side 18th Street gang member secretly for some time.

The family had the guy over to their home several times and had no problem with him—until his rival gang membership had been discovered; then, they opposed him and told the girl that she had to end her relationship with him immediately.

According to the daughter, her dad had told her that the "people on the streets" wouldn't allow the 18th Street gang member to come to their home without consequences and that she could no longer see him.

So, due to pressure from her father, she ended her relationship with the guy.

The 18th Street gang member couldn't understand why the relationship had ended, and he needed closure.

Like most men, he wanted to understand what had happened; one moment things are going fine and smooth, the next it's all over for no apparent reason.

He tried to talk to her, calling and stopping by their house, and eventually his attempts to see her became threatening.

The men in the family told him not to come back or he'd get his ass kicked, but he wasn't about to back down.

He showed up trying to talk to her, and they piled out of the house, ready to beat his ass.

The official report was that he'd driven past and shot several times into the house, then sped away.

The Youngs were hiding in the house, fearing for their lives and calling the police for help.

Bullets lodged in the interior walls of the house were recovered by CSI. That was Stils' report.

The reality, though, was entirely different.

All the men in the Young family had piled out of the house, ready to beat this guy's ass.

He'd brought a gun and flashed it, showing them that he had it and warning them to back off; however, he was outnumbered *(it was now a testosterone contest)*, so he got into his car and left the area.

He returned a short time later and shot into the house, and the Youngs returned fire, shooting at him as he drove away.

They then piled into their own cars and gave chase, shooting at him and his car as he tried to make his escape; they weren't hiding in their houses and waiting for the police to arrive.

When the initial units arrived at the Youngs' house, the brass from the family's weapons had been mostly cleaned up.

I was able to get neighbors to provide me with an account of what had really happened, but they wouldn't give a written statement; they were too afraid of what the family would do.

They also didn't trust the police to do what was right.

They felt this way because they said they'd overheard Officer Stils talking to Young, asking him to explain the expended brass he'd found in the front yard.

Young told him that his sons had fired back at the suspects from the porch—of course, leaving out the parts about the vehicle chase and firing from them.

The witnesses said that Officer Stils told Young he'd omit the part about them shooting from the porch from his report and that he'd given the brass to him and told him to get rid of it; Stils had suppressed the evidence, then wrote his report to reflect the incident the way that Young wanted.

I found the suspect, and he gave me a written confession admitting everything that the witnesses had told me.

He also told me that his younger brother had been with him and could verify everything that had happened.

I obtained a confession from the younger brother as well, and then arrested both the boyfriend and his brother.

Both were illegal aliens and were to be deported after they served their sentences.

That was one thing about the 18th Street gang that I respected: they were incredibly honest.

They admitted and owned up to everything I ever questioned them about; it was a strange characteristic unique to them.

I was able to get photos of bullet holes in the trunk of the suspect's car, as well as in the right rear quarter panel. The holes were all new and the same size.

When I asked Young point blank if he'd fired back in response to the drive by or if anyone in his family had, he became very defensive and started to attack me, stating that I was trying to damage his good name *(as if he ever had one)*.

He said that he wouldn't stand for any slander and that I and the police department had better be careful—or he'd sue us.

When I spoke to the Sergeant in charge of gangs about the case and the suppression of the evidence, he closed the door to his office and said to me, "You've got the arrest; move on. About the suppression of evidence...welcome to Detectives."

I didn't want to think about what he meant by that comment, so I talked to the county attorney handling the case and explained the suppression of the evidence.

They felt it was an internal issue that needed to be dealt with by the PD, not them, so I had no choice but to drop it.

This was my first real behind-the-scenes look at how things went in Detectives and in the county attorney's office.

It was also the first of two gang incidents I'd investigate that directly involved Councilman Young.

After I closed the case with confessions and arrests, the two suspects were easily convicted.

The Sergeant made sure that the guys who had refused to take the case while we were in Dallas were aware of that, chastising them for their refusal *(not that they cared in the slightest what he thought)*.

This didn't make me very popular with the rest of the unit.

Soon, most of the others left and went to other specialties; it wasn't easy for them to claim that their cases weren't solvable when I was solving mine.

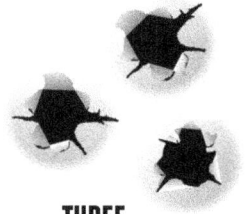

RIGHT AND WRONG?

RIGHT AND WRONG AREN'T AS obvious as some would have you think.

Looking back now, I see that more clearly.

My childhood was never ideal.

My father worked hard to provide for us, working two and sometimes three jobs to keep ahead of the constantly growing pile of bills my crazed shit storm of a mother would produce.

He wasn't a wealthy man and had only a GED, the bare minimum of education.

He wasn't stupid, though; he just had no idea what he'd married.

Quitting anything wasn't in him.

He should have walked away from the nightmare he married and taken us with him—but like I said, he had no idea how to quit.

For him, quitting was the same as failure, and he couldn't accept either.

It was really too bad because he also had no idea what went on when he wasn't at home.

I grew up being taught that it was only wrong if you got caught.

Stealing, lying, cheating—whatever fucked up thing you decided to do was fine as long as you didn't get caught. That was the value system my mother lived by and had ingrained in us, and I had no idea that it was wrong—and even less of an idea that it wasn't how the rest of the world lived.

I really had no idea that any other way even existed; I just knew how it was in my world.

Violence in the home was constant.

I remember several days when I was sure my parents would kill each other—and maybe even us.

With no moral compass to guide me and no example of what to do, I was lost—much like the people I'd run into on the street much later in life, working as a cop on the same streets I grew up in.

My mother pitted my brother and me against each other from the time we could first make a fist; I never understood how she got some sick satisfaction from the constant fighting and chaos.

Being the "wiser" and older matriarch, she'd then break up the fights and deliver our justice and punishment.

The problem was, she had a very intense need to be needed; the more she needed us, the more she provoked fights—and by the first grade, it was all-out war in our household.

We fought with weapons, hand-to-hand, and whatever we could get a hold of. Like the dogs that Michael Vick was recently arrested for fighting, we were raised to provide for her entertainment.

We were nothing more to her than those dogs were to him: mini-gladiators. In my mind, the picture seems funny; the reality, however, was not.

Here's an example of how she really was: I found out that when I was an infant *(and maybe even before I was born)* my brother was left alone with our mother.

She was evil and sadistic and would later admit to me that this incident occurred—after she'd beaten the living shit out of my brother in front of me, smashing his face into the floor repeatedly during an argument.

We were both still kids and had no idea there was anything wrong with this. It was how we grew up.

Anyway, she was kicking the hell out of him, and he said something about "remembering her smiling when he was little."

He didn't want me to know what he was talking about.

In spite of our intense hatred for each other, which was cultivated by her loving manipulation, we knew it was us against them and that they were older and stronger.

After the fight was over, I couldn't let that go...the smiling comment; I had my own fleeting memories of her smiling as well, ugly memories that I tried hard to forget.

Eventually, under the pressure of my constant questioning, she started to open up; you know the questioning that only a kid can get away with: the "Why? Why? Why? Why?"

You either get punched, or you get an answer—and I got an answer I couldn't believe...actually, I did believe it, but I didn't want to.

Turns out that when my brother was young, my dad would go to work and leave an innocent three-year-old with the woman he married. *(Nothing wrong with that in my dad's mind—what could go wrong?)*

Well, "Mary Poppins" had other ideas; she didn't want to be a mother to this child.

She was a walking nightmare of a human being, and as an adult I'd never let her spend one damn second alone with my own children until they were able to defend themselves.

Three-year-old kids are a handful, energetic, full of life, and happy. Exploring the world is what they do *(everything is new and amazing)*, and they can wear any parent down.

My mother had the coping skills of a rattlesnake: move, and she'd strike.

I don't know what my brother did; something horrendous, I'm sure, like eating too many cookies or maybe wanting a snack in the middle of her favorite fucking soap opera.

Who knows? I never asked because it didn't matter; nothing he could have done should have caused her to resort to her idea of discipline.

Years later, she admitted to me that she turned on the gas burner on the stove and lit it, then held his tiny three-year-old hand over the flame repeatedly 'til he got the message.

The comment about her smiling...well, that's what a sadistic fuck does when they harm little kids: they smile while they watch you scream in fear and pain as your flesh burns.

I listened to this and thought about the fight that I'd witnessed. As I watched his face being smashed into the floor, nothing had changed in my mind.

My brother was just bigger now, and she could no longer burn him into submission; now, she had to *beat* him into submission.

The chaos was constant, and we never knew what to expect from either of them.

Sometimes you were praised for doing well, then the very next breath you were cautioned not to get too cocky, reminded that you were nothing without their constant guidance and approval.

I realized early on that I was very much on my own.

If I were to survive this nightmare, I'd have to find another way without any help from my family.

Eventually, I realized that I could find other people who would mentor me and guide me through the tricky maze of learning about the world without any real guidance.

One night, I remember my dad asking my mom to hem some pants for him.

She didn't want to do it, and after much arguing she picked up a pair of scissors and came walking down the stairs; my mother with a weapon in her hand wasn't a thing to be taken lightly.

She had my immediate attention, and I was ready to bolt for the door, focused on her and watching her every move.

I didn't know how she'd fare in a fight against my dad; to me, it was a toss-up.

Instead of open combat, though, she picked up the pants he wanted hemmed and cut one leg completely off at the crotch.

She then said, "There you go, you son of a bitch! Now they're hemmed!"

She picked up another pair and did the same thing, then another before he finally got to her and grabbed the pants and the scissors.

They proceeded to hit each other several times, yelling names and insults, then later hugged and told each other how much they "loved" each other...this was our life.

Dad was no saint either; he had his own demons, I guess.

I never understood this incident, but it happened:

We lived in a two-story wood and brick house.

In the heat of summer, it was easily 115 degrees in my bedroom on the second floor.

At six years old, I was trying to stay cool and had stripped out of my pajamas to just my briefs.

I'd been up and down to the bathroom to wipe a wet washcloth on my chest to try to cool off and go to sleep, but it wasn't helping.

Lying in bed with nothing but a sheet, I was suddenly aware of my dad staring at me; he was smiling, but not in a happy way.

Real fear was all I felt. I'd seen this look before.

He came in and sat on the bed, then asked me what the hell I was doing *(still smiling)*. I said I was trying to keep cool.

He said, "Uh huh...sure," and pulled back the sheets. I was nearly naked underneath, so I tried to cover up.

He said, "What's the matter—are you ashamed?"

I wasn't ashamed; terrified was more like it.

He became more and more aggressive, fighting with me to try to get the sheet off the bed—but I refused to let it go; I knew it was my only protection from the attack that was about to occur.

Finally, enraged, he stood up and pulled off his belt; he'd perfected a method of getting his belt off in one move, and he was very proud of it.

Anyway, he yelled out that "no son of his was gonna be a God Damned Queer!" then proceeded to beat me with the belt until he was tired.

My mom was at the bedroom door, watching all of this—and smiling her fucking smile. Finally, even she had enough and told him to stop.

I kept the sheet tight between my hands and feet to absorb the blows; true, my hands and feet stung when they were hit, but it was all I had.

Meanwhile, I was screaming and pleading for him to stop.

Finally, exhausted, he stopped.

My mom, who had been staring at me, then shrugged her shoulders and said, "You should have known better."

At the time, I didn't know what a "queer" was, but whatever it was it had made him pretty pissed off.

A few weeks later, we got air conditioning in the house...I guess "queers" didn't like the heat.

At an age that most kids are learning about colors and numbers, I learned to swear in a way that continues to make most people gasp in shock.

Fighting was daily, either with my brother or people he set up to fight me.

I really hated fighting; it made me feel sick to be that out of control, so I also learned to run.

Later—much later—that skill would take me to the High School State Cross Country championships my senior year, where I'd place 6th in the entire state.

I wasn't a runner by any stretch of the imagination; however, I had an enormous reservoir of rage to tap into when the pain started to flow through my body during the all-out-fast-as-you-can-run race.

The coach *(one of many mentors)* must have recognized this early on.

He took me aside before our first real race, away from the squeaky clean church boys I ran with, and told me, "I see that you go out way too damn fast at first, and you're running in oxygen debt for three quarters of the race. Hold back 'til I tell you to go, OK?"

I said that I only knew one way to run.

It was true.

I'd learned to run to survive: flat out, haul ass, then hold on and outlast your enemy. Endurance has been a gift my whole life.

He held me really firmly by both shoulders, stared at me a moment, then said, "I know how you run, and I know why. Do what I tell you. Wait for my word, and then you can run like you want to. Deal?"

We stared at each other for a few seconds.

I didn't know what he knew or how he knew it, but I agreed. It would be hard, but I could try it.

I started the race last man on Junior Varsity.

I was our worst runner by far; I was way too big and heavy to run with any of those clean cut, skinny church boys. They read scriptures, and I cut class.

I had long hair past my shoulders, and they had their short missionary haircuts.

Needless to say, I wasn't one of them, so I have to admit the idea of beating their church-going asses made me really happy, only I hadn't been able to—yet.

Anyway, the race started, and I did what the coach asked, holding back and feeling like I was gonna die.

Running like that caused me a lot of anxiety, whereas running was usually freedom for me; the faster I ran, the better I felt. *(In my mind, it meant I didn't have to fight—and I liked that.)*

As I was holding back and waiting, I started to have adrenaline dumps like crazy.

This had been my survival mechanism for years, and now I was crawling, hanging back in the pack with the slowest guys.

At the mile mark, I was suddenly aware of the coach running next to me.Barely breathing, he said, "Are you ready now?"

I said, "Ya."

He said, "OK. Open it up slowly, then let go and fly. I'll see you at the finish line."

I looked at him, and he smiled and said, "Go, Zach, go!"

Two miles later, with pain raging through my body like I'd only experienced in a real battle for survival, I crossed the finish line—coming in third on the team.

Even though I was 25 pounds heavier than anyone else on Varsity, I'd smoked the entire team except for the two absolute best runners.

One of them would become a world-class distance runner in college, the other was to be a good friend all through high school.

I've heard that Malcolm X once said, "Anger is a gift"; well, I've carried this "gift" my whole life—that and an intense desire to make shit that's obviously wrong, right again.

Why do I tell you all of this?

Because all of these experiences made me better on the street.

I learned early that nothing is what it seems. Leaders rarely have your best interests at heart.

Just because people go to church and put on smiles for the neighbors, it doesn't mean they're good people.

Not all parents "love" their kids.

Kids are products of where they come from; they don't just become killers—they're made into killers.

I used my life, my experiences, and my rage to relate to the people in the streets.

The gang members, hood rats, and drug dealers—the shit of society, all came from one form of dysfunction or another, and so did I.

Maybe some of them did truly have good families, but they themselves had a mental illness. I'd witnessed that as well, from day one of my life.

Sometimes a person from a bad parenting environment could survive and become more than their surroundings, excelling *in spite* of their environment and parents.

I tried to find those people and help them like I'd been helped.

I had the debt of surviving my childhood to pay forward to someone else, and I did what I could do...sometimes I succeeded.

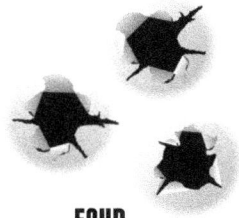

SPEAK ENGLISH, DAMN IT

ABOUT MID-BLOCK ON 38TH STREET, just above Adams Ave. on the north side, was a dead end street.

It had several rundown rental units that populated the inner city; landlords would rent them out to people who were just shy of being homeless: the throwaways of the city, the disposable people.

They're there in every city; maybe you see them, maybe you don't. They're the people whom no one wants or they try hard to ignore.

Anyway, it went back in about halfway into the block, ending in an overgrown field. There was a family there that rented one of the units. They were Hispanic; they'd come from Mexico with their kids and were trying to start over and build a better life.

The parents both worked two full-time jobs, each at a fast food restaurant, while the older kids took care of the younger kids.

Theirs was a typical immigrant story in America: one generation after another working hard to make a better life for their kids.

One day, their son Alex and his cousin Jose had taken the family's only car for a joy ride. The parents were unaware of this.

The boys, each fifteen years old, were on an adventure; however, when they returned home they'd been the victims of a drive-by shooting, having been ambushed at an intersection while they waited for the light to change by two guys they knew from high school.

Alex and Jose had been heading southbound on Field Ave. when they came to a stoplight at the corner of 34th. Arturo Laredo and a friend were driving in the area and saw the Ornelas driving.

According to the Ornelas, they were enemies; they were rivals in school and on the street.

I didn't know it at the time, but the Ornelas were South Side 18th Street. I knew that Laredo was St. Pauls 13.

So, as Alex Ornelas was stopped at the light, Laredo told his friend Manuel Moncada to slowly pull up alongside him, driving in the oncoming lane.

He then hung out of the passenger side of the car and shot at the Ornelas several times, hitting Alex and narrowly missing his cousin.

Laredo emptied the gun into the driver's side of the car, shooting through the driver's open window at point blank range, then left the area.

Afterwards, Alex and Jose went home as fast as they could. This was all done in broad daylight, close to noon, just outside the struggling St. Pauls City Mall.

I was sent to the dead end street to assist the rest of the Gang Task Force in investigating the shooting.

When I arrived at the half street, I found the Ornelas family in a frantic mess. The parents spoke very little English and were trying to tell dispatchers that their son had been shot.

I arrived as Sergeant Gus, the Gang Task Force Sergeant at the time, Mike Vetere, and Noah Clark were also arriving.

We all got out and tried to sort out what had happened, unaware that this was to be a quick reality check of why the Gang Task Force wasn't solving cases.

Being the alleged leader of our group, Sergeant Gus asked the parents what had happened.

He didn't speak Spanish, and he didn't believe that they didn't speak English.

When they tried to tell him what had happened, he became really confrontational and told them that he knew they spoke English and that this "Yo no hablo bullshit" wasn't going to work with him.

He yelled at the parents and repeatedly told them that we weren't going to help if they didn't start speaking English—and fast.

Meanwhile, their son was bleeding and going into shock, and Medical still hadn't arrived.

I listened to Gus, Clark, and Vetere berate and insult these people for about two minutes, then I'd finally had enough.

I said to Gus, "Who's taking this case?"

Gus looked at me and asked what I meant, so I said to him, "Who are you gonna assign this case to? Because I'm outta here if all you're gonna do is talk shit to these people. I still have the Young shooting that I need to work on; if you aren't gonna get anywhere with these people, then I have shit to do."

Gus glared at me, then said, "OK then, smart ass, *you* get the case. It's all yours."

He then asked me in a really condescending tone, "What would you like us to do, Detective?"

This just pissed me off even more.

I said, "I want you to leave before you fuck this up worse than you already have. You can't insult the fucking victims and expect them to cooperate in your case."

While Vetere and Clark started glaring at me, giving me dirty looks, Gus thought this over for a minute, then smiled *(one of those "plotting against you" kind of smiles)* and said, "OK. What can I do to help?"

I needed the car processed for evidence, as well as the names of the people who were present, and he tasked Vetere and Clark with those jobs.

In turn, they did the bare minimum that each task required and handed the information over to me.

The Three Amigos then turned and walked away from the scene, their fat asses wobbling down the one-way street, returning to the world where drive-bys didn't occur—and if they did, no one talked about them.

Evidently, their help in this case was done.

As they left, I heard Gus say to Vetere, "We'll see how cocky he is after he gets his ass reamed for not solving this one."

Vetere laughed in agreement, saying, "Those fucking Mexicans are gonna make him look stupid. Everyone knows they can speak English, and besides they probably caused this damn shooting themselves. You know they're lying about this shit; they just hide it to get one over on us."

The injured Alex Ornelas was transported to the hospital for treatment.

He had a bullet wound in the leg, but it wasn't life-threatening.

I asked him if he knew who had shot him, and he said that it was Arturo Laredo, who he'd known from school; he was positive it was Laredo.

I knew who Laredo was, and I went back to the office and started to try to throw together a photo lineup.

Since he went straight to surgery, it would be several hours before I could run the photo lineup past the boy.

I called dispatch to get the time that the incident was reported, as well as the case number.

They told me that just as the shooting had been reported at the residence, another shooting had been reported by a woman who said she'd witnessed a drive-by shooting at the mall.

They sent patrols to the scene, but they'd found nothing. She'd left her name and information, and they'd assign it to me if I thought the shootings were related.

I wrote down the woman's information and called her.

It seemed unlikely that the shootings *wouldn't* be related; however, shootings happened often enough in the city, and quite often more than one shooting or incident was going on at the same time.

It was never safe to assume anything...ever.

I arranged to go to her house and meet with her.

When I arrived, she was a wreck; she was crying and sobbing and had really been traumatized by the incident.

She said that she'd been going to the mall with her daughter to spend the Saturday shopping and hanging out; they'd planned to try on clothes and have a nice Mother-Daughter day.

They turned the corner at 34th and Field, just as Arturo Laredo had started to hang out the passenger side of the car he was in.

She said that she saw everything.

She recalled every shot, as well as the "evil" look on Arturo's face as he shot into the Ornelas' car; she described the look as "filled with hate and rage," and she'd never seen that look on anyone in her life.

She said that she was in the way of Arturo's escape from the scene.

Since he'd pulled up alongside the vehicle the Ornelas were in, he was in the northbound side, blocking her lane.

They stared at each other for a few moments, and she was terrified that Laredo was going to get out of the car and shoot her and her daughter as well.

The driver of Laredo's car, however, did find a way past her, and they drove off and left the area.

I asked her if she had a description of the car, and she recalled it well. It was a small white car, and she'd written down the license plate.

I couldn't believe it. In any incident, it's really rare that a witness has the ability to remember to get real, useable information; usually, they're in such a state of shock that any memory is gone in moments.

I took the paper that she'd written the plate down on and asked her if there was anything else that she could remember.

She said, "Yes, the two boys in the other car, the car that was shot at, did nothing to provoke this shooting. They were ambushed by this evil man."

She would be an incredible witness.

I went back to the police department and announced the information I had on the radio in an ATL *(attempt to locate)*.

Sergeant Gus then approached me and told me that he'd assigned to me a guy named Dave Magnum; he was on loan from the County Sheriff, and we were supposed to go out and patrol the central city area, look for possible gang parties, and break them up.

I asked him, "What about the active shooting case I'm working on?"

As if he were surprised, he said, "Oh yeah...you can work on that, too, I guess!"

I was starting to get into a slow, burning mental rage.

The lack of desire by the rest of the unit to work these cases to an arrest and conviction was really getting to me; there was no sense of urgency or ownership to any of this.

I went out with Magnum and began to look for the shooters; fuck the parties the Sergeant wanted us to hit.

I'd worked with Magnum at the county when I was there.

He was a really nice guy, but he wasn't forceful and definitely had no feel for the street.

He was the kind of guy you wanted as a neighbor, not as back up in a fight; he'd wilt like a flower in the glaring sun at the first sign of confrontation.

We drove around for about half an hour, with me seething about the stupid shit I was seeing in the unit; I was mumbling to myself about how fucking dumb it was to send me out to look for parties when people were in armed combat at the mall in broad daylight.

Magnum took this personally and said that I could take him back to the station if I wanted; he didn't want to disobey an order from the Sergeant and was passively telling me that he wanted to go back to the station if we weren't going to do exactly what we were told.

I was considering taking his candy ass back when we pulled up to the intersection of 59th and Orchard.

I sat there for a minute, looking east and west; I don't know why I sat there, but I did.

This would happen a lot to me when I was in gangs.

I'd suddenly get an overwhelming feeling that I needed to go somewhere, or sometimes—like this day—just sit and wait. Call it a hunch or a gut feeling; I just felt I had to wait.

We sat there for a few moments, then finally Magnum said to me, "Hey man, are we gonna go?"

I said, "Ya, ya...in a second."

After a minute of waiting at the stop sign, a car pulled up behind us and honked.

Still, I sat...something was coming; I could feel it.

Then I saw a small white car coming towards us down the hill, and I said to Magnum, "Look what we have here: a small white car."

As it got closer, I could see two occupants, then the license plate; it was a match to the plate that I'd been given by the witness to the shooting.

Magnum looked at me in disbelief, his jaw dropped open with a "WTF" look in his eyes.

I told him that this was the suspect vehicle in my shooting case and that we were going to pull it over.

Swallowing in fear, he almost whispered, "Shouldn't we wait for back up?"

I said, "Fuck that! Surprise is on our side."

I then called out on the radio that I had the vehicle in the shooting at the mall and gave out our location.

We did a felony stop, my way. *(My way of a felony stop wasn't the typical tactics you're taught in the Academy. I like to get up close and personal; I want to see what's going on in the car and be sure that if I have to shoot someone—I hit them.)*

I approached any car with my gun out and aimed at the driver's head, letting them know in no uncertain terms that I'll kill them if they get stupid; this way, I'm able to see everything they do and every move they make, and there are no surprises.

This is not at all what you're taught in the Academy; however, as most cops who have been in the shit storm that's the streets know, the Academy is just a frame of reference. It isn't the end, but the beginning of your tactical training; you must always keep learning and adjusting to your environment.

Magnum wasn't happy about this.

As we approached, I had my weapon out and pointed at the driver, calmly telling him that if he made any move that I didn't tell him to make—today would be his last day; meanwhile, Magnum was doing the usual "Hi, I'm Officer Dave Magnum, may I see your ID" routine that we use on the mom-and-pop traffic stop.

I yelled at him to wake the fuck up and get his gun out on his suspect.

These two guys were wanted for a shooting and would kill him in a second if he slipped up. They'd already shot one guy that day, and they were probably still armed.

Magnum finally realized that he wasn't in the "green acres" anymore and geared up as much as he could.

We removed the two suspects and put them in cuffs, then searched them for weapons and found none.

Just then, Vetere and Clark showed up.

They offered to help out, so I asked them to process the car and impound it as evidence; I wanted the car searched for the gun as well. They did the impound sheet while Magnum and I went to the station with the suspects.

I interviewed the two suspects, but I wasn't able to get a confession from either one; I was, though, able to establish an alibi that was very easy to defeat.

The two men claimed that they'd been at Arturo's house, watching "The Untouchables."

They said that they'd been there for a few hours, watching the movie. They'd planned an alibi, but when separated neither one could recall what the movie was about, who the characters were, who died in the movie, or what the ending was.

I yelled at them out of frustration, telling them, "How fucking dumb can you two be? You come up with an alibi of watching this movie—and you pick one that neither of you has ever actually watched? You're fucking idiots!"

I booked them both into jail for the shooting, basing the arrest on the positive identification by the victims, as well as the identification of the car and Laredo by the woman going shopping at the mall.

The failed interviews of the two men took several hours.

I had to deal with constant interference from Vetere and Clark, who cracked jokes, talked about what they ate for dinner, and did their best to make sure that I couldn't get a confession.

The idea in interviewing is to keep up the pressure on your suspects, allowing them no way out and nowhere to hide from the facts that you're presenting. Eventually, they see they have no choice but to confess, and when you get them to that point, you offer an alternative, a way for this to "not be all their fault."

It doesn't have to make sense; it just has to allow them an escape from the emotional pressure that you're putting on them.

It really works well; however, it doesn't work at all when there are distractions that deflect the focus of the suspect from his troubles to anything else.

Having learned my lesson on this case, from then on I interviewed alone in a small plain room with no one else and nothing but the suspects and me; this allowed them nowhere to hide and nowhere to go.

It was really late, nearly 3a.m., when we had it all wrapped up for the night.

As we sat in the gang office, we breathed a sigh of relief.

The gang unit was looked upon as a joke; they couldn't solve cases, couldn't get convictions, and the poorest detectives ended up there—not by their choice, but by their failures.

Unlike the rest of the guys in the unit, though, I'd chosen to go there; I liked working gangs.

Anyway, Gus was our Sergeant, and he was debriefing us, making sure he had all the details of the shoot and the arrests before he called the Duty Lieutenant, who had just gotten off about two hours before. He made some notes and then made the call.

Gus thought of himself as an efficiency expert.

He had all kinds of phone lists miniaturized and laminated in his wallet, and he pulled one out and showed it to us, making sure we saw how efficient he was.

We all rolled our eyes and waited for him to finish while he called the number.

He thought he was calling his friend Lt. James, the Duty Lieutenant, but instead he'd called Chief James—and they were most definitely *not* friends.

Chief James and Gus had competed for the Chief spot when it had come open about eight months earlier; Chief James had won, and Gus had lost.

They'd been adversaries within the department for years.

Gus thought of himself as the intellectual, whereas Chief James claimed to be a "military man" by way of his Army reserve experience. They couldn't have been more opposite in their outlook or approach to police work.

Chief James hated Gus, who was overweight and a prankster, never serious and always joking.

He even moonlighted as a comedian at a club on Elm Street.

Chief James never laughed...ever.

So Gus called who he thought was Lieutenant James and started his usual joking and shit talking, saying that he was surprised that Lt. James was asleep—and already referring to him as "James."

He made several comments about James "banging his new girl-friend, and that must be why he's so tired," asking if she was as hot as she appeared to be.

He made comments about how he imagined she was in bed (*Lt. James had recently divorced his wife and was seeing a dispatcher, who we all heard was very wild*), then he proceeded to talk shit on Chief James—still not realizing that was, in fact, who he was talking to.

He said, "At least you're not at home with a ball gag in your mouth, taking it up the ass like the Chief; his wife runs that fucking house. You know she has to have a strap-on in the drawer by the bed. Probably never uses Vaseline either—just the way the Chief likes it."

Gus was laughing at the picture he painted, thinking it was quite funny—then all at once his demeanor changed, and he sat right up and said, "Yes, sir,", then "Yes, sir!" again and gave a quick brief of the shoot, apologizing for the inconvenience.

Gus then hung up, went completely pale, put his head down on the desk, and said, "Fellahs, I am so fucked! Oh God, I am so fucked!"

He was always pulling pranks, so we didn't believe his change of demeanor.

Seeing that we weren't buying into this, he stood up and yelled, "This is *not* fucking funny! I'm serious."

Still not believing him, we asked what had happened, and he said that he'd mistakenly called Chief James instead of Lieutenant James.

We all looked at each other in shock, thinking about what he'd said in that conversation—then we burst out laughing.

We laughed so hard, we started to grab garbage cans because we were throwing up.

Gus just stormed out of the office, pissed off.

He left us there, dry heaving with tears running down our faces, laughing and gagging.

Gus and the Chief had many funny conversations, and Gus' sense of humor got the best of him many times.

When this case went to court, the driver, Manuel Moncada, pled guilty and was convicted easily.

Laredo, on the other hand, didn't go down without a fight.

He requested a jury trial, and his parents mortgaged their business and house to ensure that they could get him cleared of the charges.

After three days of trial, the jury returned a guilty verdict in a few hours.

His family went crazy and began yelling at me that I was fucking dead and was gonna get mine.

A few weeks later, they accused me of tampering with the jury, claiming that I had contact with one of the jury members.

I had to go back to court and try to figure out what the hell they were talking about.

The allegations weren't true; it turned out that I'd been talking to the victims' assistance coordinator, and they thought she was a jury member.

The conviction held, and Laredo went to prison.

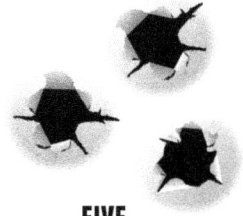

CAPPED IN THE ASS

YOU KNOW HOW YOU HEAR about bangers always talking shit about "bustin' caps in some fool's ass"? Well, sometimes they mean it!

Doughboy from St. Pauls 13 had just come home on a home visit. He'd been in a Proctor home in San Marcos by court order, and he was allowed to go home on rare occasions to see his mom.

He'd been home in the city less than twenty-four hours when this shooting happened. *(It's also noteworthy that while he was in San Marcos, they had numerous drive-by shootings and gang activity increased noticeably...hmm...wonder why that was?)*

Anyway, Doughboy met up with Roberto Vega, another SP-13 gang member who had been in another "rehab program" back east.

They hung out at Vega's house, playing video games for a while, then decided go for a walk to another friend's house.

Both Vega and Doughboy had been out of the city for several months, so they went out walking in their old neighborhoods, talking about the girls they'd met during the time they'd been gone and comparing notes on their latest sexual conquests.

Suddenly, they ran into several South Side 18th Street gang members, Neto Arredondo and his cousins.

Arredondo was South Side 18th Street and had it tattooed on his chest. He was very proud of his gang membership, but his parents hoped it was a phase that he would soon outgrow.

This particular day, his family was having a wedding. His sister was getting married, and he and his cousins had come to the house to get wedding decorations.

They were standing in the front yard of Arredondo's house, taking a smoke break from loading their truck.

As Doughboy and Vega walked by, the two groups exchanged words.

It started out with "Whatchu claim, man", then went downhill fast from there. They were sworn rivals who hated each other by their gang affiliations.

Doughboy was a huge kid; at sixteen, he looked like a 35-year-old man. He was 5'8" and easily 250 lb.—and he feared no one on the streets.

He was one of only two Black kids that claimed St. Pauls 13 at the time; the other was already in prison for a shooting.

Black kids in St. Pauls 13 were rare since it was a Hispanic gang homegrown and unique to St. Pauls.

Most Black gang members in the city ended up as Crips or Bloods; Dough, however, had grown up hanging out with the homegrown Hispanics and felt an allegiance both to them and the Blacks in the city. He was a very unique guy in a lot of ways.

Anyway, Doughboy jumped the small fence in the front of the house and called the Arredondos out to fight.

St. Pauls 13 called the 18th Street gang members "in-betweeners" and sometimes "sewer rats"; 18th Street, on the other hand, called the SP-13 members "Chochas", "Dirtheads", or "Fakers."

So, Doughboy challenged the "sewer rats" to a fight.

The South Side 18th Street members outnumbered him, but he was huge—and he could fight.

The 18th Street members kept talking shit to him as they backed away, telling him to get the fuck off their property and get the fuck out of there.

Meanwhile, Arredondo went around the back of the house and went inside to get his father's 44 mag.

He then came out the front door of the house and confronted Dough, telling him to "get the fuck off of his property" or he'd kill him.

Doughboy called his bluff and stood his ground, talking shit back to Arredondo and telling him that he was going to kick his ass for trying to scare him with some fake ass gun.

That was a huge mistake—because Arredondo wasn't bluffing.

He shot one round at Doughboy's head, narrowly missing it; the round ended up burying itself deep into the telephone pole behind Doughboy and to his left.

At that point, Doughboy quickly realized that maybe it was time to leave, so he turned and tried to run, jumping the short fence with Arredondo in pursuit.

Doughboy took a couple steps, and Arredondo shot again; this time, he hit Dough right in the ass, the bullet driving deep into the muscle of his right ass cheek.

The bullet's impact was so forceful; it knocked Dough right out of his shoes.

Still, he continued running as fast as he could, limping now and bleeding.

Arredondo shot one more round at Dough as he ran past another telephone pole, again narrowly missing his head; the third round also got buried in the telephone pole.

Meanwhile, Vega was in high-speed "get the hell out of Dodge mode," running as fast as he could from the area.

He wanted nothing to do with the fight; he was on probation and nowhere near the soldier that Doughboy was on the street.

Vega never looked back, leaving Doughboy wounded, bleeding, and running for his life.

Asshole and elbows was all Doughboy saw; Vega was gone, leaving him to live or die on his own.

After yelling out threats and challenges to the neighborhood, Arredondo put the gun back in the house, announcing, "No one had better fuck with 18th Street!"

He then continued on to his sister's wedding like nothing had ever happened, feeling satisfied that he'd made his point, shooting one of the St. Pauls 13 gang bangers and sending the other running for his life.

As far as he was concerned, he'd shown—for that day, anyway—that South Side 18th Street is not to be fucked with. His cousins began praising him for his shooting of the "fakers," and for the time being he was the hero.

Doughboy, meanwhile, had run down the avenue away from the gunfire and eventually got some help from an elderly Black man who saw him limping and bleeding, trying to escape from Arredondo.

The man brought him into his own home, then drove him to the hospital to be treated. He didn't call for the police; calling the police in that neighborhood wasn't even considered an option.

I got the report of the shooting in the area, and when I arrived nothing was there and no one remained.

No one waved me down; people just stared, watching and saying nothing.

I had to walk the neighborhood and search for people willing to talk to me. Finally, I started to get witnesses talking and put together what had happened.

I was there for some time, winning back the neighborhood.

I found the shoes that belonged to Doughboy, and with the witnesses' help I had a pretty good idea of what had happened—I just didn't know why.

Then I got a call that a Black male had arrived at a nearby hospital, shot in the buttocks, so I headed up there to see if the call that I was on and the injured male in the hospital were related.

I met with Doughboy in the Emergency Room.

I'd known him for several years already, and we had a really good relationship. He knew me from patrol, and I'd picked him up for previous gang detectives many times.

I'd always treated him with respect and often took him to get a soft drink and say goodbye to his mother the times that I picked him up; this meant a lot to him and his mom.

I asked Doughboy what had happened to him, and he told me all about the incident.

He told me about Vega and Arredondo and the 18th Street bangers in front of the house. He was completely straightforward about what had happened.

I obtained a statement from him about what had happened, then went back to the scene.

Before I left, I teased him a bit about the gunshot to the ass, and we laughed.

Usually, bangers would be proud of the scar a gunshot would produce and would show it off to their friends at parties. I joked with him that he'd be showing off his ass at SP-13 parties and that no one would wanna see it.

We laughed about this for a while. Then I left the Emergency Room.

I went back to the scene and talked to Arredondo's parents, who had just arrived home from the wedding, and explained what had happened.

The said that they didn't know where Neto was, but when he returned they'd bring him to me. They were very upset about the situation and said that he'd brought shame to the family name.

To make matters worse, he'd done this at their home and on their daughter's wedding day. They were very upset by the incident.

I gave them my phone number and asked them to call when he returned, then left the residence.

I returned to the station and briefed Sergeant Gus about what I'd found out, telling him that the Arredondo family said they'd call when Neto came home.

He rolled his eyes and said that I was "stupid to believe a bunch of fucking Mexicans."

He then said to me, "Man, where the hell have you been the last few years? Working in fucking Mayberry?"

I tried to explain to him that the Arredondo family was old school Mexico and that they had the old school Mexican values. I believed them when they said they'd be in with Neto when he came home; this was a point of honor for the entire family.

Gus shook his head and said that I "had a lot to learn about Mexicans."

I was getting really pissed, so I replied, "If I'm so fucking dumb about the street, how come I've solved the past two cases you gave me with arrests—while no one else in this unit has solved shit for months?"

He got up, mumbling something about "smart ass rookie," then left the office.

I started on my case report, and a couple hours later when I was almost done, the entire Arredondo family showed up with Neto.

They'd told him that he'd better confess to everything that had happened, or he'd be banished from the family and no longer considered a part of them.

He did confess to everything and told me the same story that Doughboy had recounted in the Emergency Room.

His father came to me afterwards and wanted to make sure that I was satisfied with the confession. He personally apologized for his son's behavior and said that he hoped that I'd call on him if I needed anything else for the case.

He said that he wouldn't have his family name tarnished by this incident and that his son would make this right or be forever banished from the family.

This was impressive shit to me, but not uncommon with families coming from Mexico that had the "old school" value system.

That was how every old school family I ever met from Mexico was; their family name and honor was everything to them. I had tremendous respect for the Arredondos.

Neto was just a juvenile at the time, but he was eventually certified as an adult and sent to prison.

When we went to court on the case, Doughboy was brought back to St .Pauls from San Marcos, where he'd returned after the shooting.

He didn't know who the guy was who had shot him, but when we went to court and he saw Arredondo and heard his name, he recognized him from high school and middle school.

Doughboy was shocked; he told me that he'd been friends with Arredondo in school for years.

He said, "Damn, this shit is stupid! We were friends in school. I didn't recognize him that day, and now we're in court."

He was genuinely upset, but not enough to leave the gang life.

As for Neto, though, I heard through the 18th Street members that he swore off the gang life and totally left it.

In letters from prison, he told them that he wouldn't be a member anymore and that he had to get his life back on track. He had to choose between his family and his gang—and he chose family.

He was lucky that his family was so strict in their belief that he had to make this right.

I never saw him again, even after he got out of prison. As far as I know, that was the end of his gang affiliation.

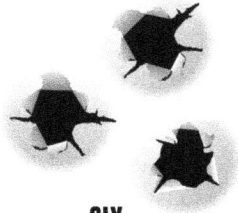

ST. PAUL'S TRECE GANG

I FIRST MET DOUGHBOY, THE Laredo brothers, and the majority of the peewee St. Pauls Trece gang members at Sam Ochoa's house in the 2200 block of St. Pauls Ave.

Sam and his older brother Jim were the nephews of the alleged leaders of St. Pauls 13. They claimed that their uncles "Getback", "Kickback", and "Shady" started SP-13 from CCL *(Central City Lobos)*.

From what I could figure out through interviews and filling in the blanks, some of the CCL gang members had gone to prison and met up there with other gang members from Sureneos 13.

In the prison system, the number 13 stands for the 13th letter of the alphabet: "M" *(for Eme, meaning the Mexican Mafia)*.

The southern California gangs have a huge influence on prison culture, and soon all the Sureneos gangs identified with the number 13.

The incarcerated CCL members came out of prison and adopted the 13 to their gang, adding the city name or initials.

They then spread the word and started St. Pauls 13. CCL was now only the older guys, and St. Pauls 13 was born.

I don't know for sure that the Ochoa family started SP-13; it's complicated because SP-13 is made up of several families and is organized more like a terrorist organization than a typical gang with a tree-like hierarchy *(leaders, captains, mid-level leaders, gang bangers, and peewees)*; instead, SP-13 has cells, families that are aligned with each other—and in some cases, rivals.

It's unlike any other gang in St. Pauls.

SP-13 gang members will fight each other and snitch on each other if they're from rival cells, and its gang membership isn't limited to members who live in St Pauls; they live all around the surrounding areas.

Additionally, SP-13 members don't have to be from one of the original families or from a specific race. Their membership includes blacks, whites, and members from other states who have moved into the city.

Another thing unique to SP-13 is that none of the junior members have any idea of the history behind their name or how the gang is organized; they're culturally unaware of the beginnings of the gang or the symbolism of the "13" in the name of the gang.

There are six main families that I could identify in the gang, and they're each unaware of what the other family cells are doing. It's a loose organization, and that's why it's so hard to defeat.

The police department has never addressed the cell organization; it treats the gang like a unified organization—which it is *not*.

If they addressed each family cell and organized their investigations based on that, the gang would quickly disappear.

I wrote an intelligence case to keep this knowledge of the structure of the gang in the database of the police department, but I doubt it's ever been viewed or acknowledged; that kind of intel wasn't seen as useful by the department's leadership.

I met a lot of the peewee SP-13 gang members at the Ochoa house. They initially didn't like me because I was a cop—and the feeling was mutual; I hated gang members with a passion. Since their mom worked, the Ochoa boys were unsupervised in the daytime.

I had no idea where their father was, and I never asked. It was obvious he wasn't in the picture. All I knew was that they never mentioned him, and he was never around.

The other peewees would show up at the house in the summer and raise hell with the neighbors, throwing rocks at cars and flashing gang signs.

They'd often try to pick fights with the Job Corps kids, who were let off at an office building across the street that was an annex for that program.

It was a really good idea for me to hang close to the Ochoa house when I was in patrol and stop fights and criminal mischief before it got started.

This was where I developed the strategy that would enable me to close the majority of my cases, develop informants, and get gang members to testify against each other in court.

One day while talking shit to the peewees at the Ochoa house, exchanging insults and name-calling, I noticed one of the kids was listening to the exchange; laughing but not angry, he had a lonely look in his eyes.

I watched him intently and noticed that he was really interested in the way that the police car was arranged inside. He was always looking in the windows, smiling and looking around, but he never said a word.

Eventually, I asked him if he wanted to see how the lights and sirens worked.

He said nothing, but his eyes lit up.

I turned them on, both lights and sirens—and the spell was instantly broken with all the peewees; in a single moment, they were transformed from hateful, spiteful, angry wannabe gang members into happy, laughing, normal acting kids.

They all came running and commenting on how cool the lights and sirens were, asking if they could turn them on, how it all worked, and what it was like to be a cop.

I was completely shocked at the transformation, and I had a hard time talking to them as the children they now were, remembering the hateful looks I was being given just moments before.

But the spell was broken for them and for me, and I let them take turns turning on the lights and sirens. Later, I even took the Ochoa boys for a ride in the car.

This was an epiphany, a turning point, as I realized that gang members had a real weakness.

The streets had hardened them.

They'd been twisted and screwed up by bad families, poor parenting, and the feeling that no one cared.

They were programmed to be able to defend themselves against anger, rage, and violence, but they had no defense against kindness, respect, or friendship. This formed the basic principals I used to develop informants and solve cases.

I treated all of them—no matter how much I disliked them—with respect and kindness, praising what I saw they took pride in, no matter how insignificant it appeared.

They all craved attention like every other person, maybe even more so.

Most cops treated them harshly, but they were able to defeat that; the more harshly they were treated, the stronger they were against the attack. But they had no defenses against kindness.

The younger kid who wanted to see the lights and so badly needed attention was a pivotal moment for me.

At the time, the group at the Ochoa house were just kids; they later grew up to be hardcore gangbangers, very capable of crimes and killing.

This group of kids would later be huge in the gang culture of the city. They included Arturo and Juan Laredo, Steve Costa, Sam and Jim Ochoa, Doughboy and Andrew Lucero *(li'l man)*, and Anthony Green.

Green, the only other Black kid in St. Pauls 13, was sent to prison at eighteen for an aggravated robbery. He lived with his grandmother, and she seemed resigned to the fact that he was gone forever when he was locked up. I tried to talk to her about him, and she gave me this look that said she was done with him, then closed the door on me.

He joined a Blood set just before he went to prison; being Black, he believed he couldn't belong to St. Pauls 13 in prison and have any protection, so he "jumped sets."

I asked the St. Pauls 13 gang members I knew about this, and they didn't deny that he'd jumped sets or that he'd have no protection.

This proved to me more the reality of what I saw in gang membership: the loyalty they claimed to feel for each other and the gang was fleeting at best.

A few years later, I saw his obituary in the summer; he was dead at an age when most men are just starting their own families.

Gangbangers live fast and hard, and they almost always die early.

GANG LIFE: THE PAINFUL REALITY

I FIRST MET STEVE FLOREZ Costa in the Gang Task Force office.

He'd been arrested for aggravated assault by Det. Dave Sessions, who'd survived the second "purge" of the gang unit by the Police Administration.

Purging the detectives from the task force was the administration's way of dealing with the gang problem; they purged the unit, removing all officers they felt were ineffective—whenever the prevailing political winds started to heat up.

City Council members who had absolutely no idea of the street, police work, or gangs would decide to flex their muscle with the Police Chief, asking what he'd done to increase gang suppression. Instead of finding a real fix for the problem, like adding more officers motivated to deal with the issue intelligently, or programs to help kids out with alternatives to gang life, he'd bring pressure on the Sergeant and Lieutenant to make personnel changes in the unit.

This was a quick fix that looked good on paper politically, but it did nothing to address the issue. It happened time and time again, usually every two years or so.

Anyway, Costa was the typical angry gang member; he was pissed off, abusive, and talking shit to Sessions and any other cop who came in to the office.

As I watched him and tried to learn about him, I saw that he was acting just like the peewee gang members and that he had the same defense mechanisms. He lashed out at everyone, and he was angry and spiteful to anyone who walked in or was nearby.

Sessions had called his parents, and they came down to say goodbye to Steve; he was going to jail, then most likely to prison after trial.

Sessions liked the parents and had developed a good relationship with them, so he left the room and let them have a moment alone with Steve. I stayed in the room to make sure he didn't escape, so I overheard their conversation.

Unhappy with his gang membership, they were basically telling him that he was on his own from now on.

His stepfather told him that Steve had wanted this life, that he had a choice and could have chosen another life—but didn't. Now he'd have to face the consequences of his decision.

His stepfather said that he was embarrassed to have called Steve his son and that as long as he maintained his membership in the gang, he wasn't welcome in their home. They were cutting ties with him as I listened.

Crying and furious, Steve told his stepfather he'd never understand what it meant to be a "soldier." He said that he was going to be a part of something bigger than his stepfather's piss poor life; he'd be a legend in the prison system, respected and admired as an OG *(original gangster)*.

He said that when they heard about how respected he was by the inmates and gang members on the street, they'd beg for him to return to the family. He'd show them they were wrong.

He told his stepfather to go fuck himself, then he let his mother hug him goodbye. They left the room, and Sessions came back and booked Costa into the jail.

Costa was released from prison in the late 1990s, being let out on parole.

I met him again when I was sent as a backing unit to a burglary alarm at Big O Tires.

It was in an affluent part of town with nice homes and clean parks, and gang crime wasn't supposed to occur in this world.

We never received alarms from the businesses in the area that weren't legit, so we approached this one with caution.

The business had been broken into; when we arrived, we were able to find the broken window that had been used to enter the business.

We surrounded the place and waited for K-9 to arrive.

As we were waiting, a guy jumped out from a large bush in the manicured landscaping near the business and broke into a run.

We chased him down and pepper sprayed him, and he went down fast as the spray took effect.

It was winter, and snow was on the ground, so we treated him with the snow until medical arrived to treat the effects of the pepper spray.

Once he calmed down and sat up, I recognized him as Costa.

He was much older looking, severely tattooed, and he was still just as angry and spiteful as he'd been before—perhaps even more.

After getting him calmed down, we found out he was on paper *(parole)* and that he was intoxicated; this alone violated his parole.

We had CSI process the scene at the business, and in the meantime we took Costa to the station for interviewing.

Costa's story was that he'd been at a SP-13 party.

He'd been invited as an OG who had just been released from prison and had arrived expecting to be admired and respected; instead, he was challenged, insulted, and belittled.

He didn't know what to think.

The junior members had shown him absolutely no respect at all, challenging him to a fight and talking shit about him being an "old man" and having no heart.

To prove his continued loyalty to the gang, they challenged him to participate in the business burglary.

He eagerly agreed, and when they arrived Costa took the initiative in entering the building.

What he didn't know was that things on the street had changed since he'd entered prison.

Senior gang members like Costa were no longer respected for what they had been; they had to re-establish their position in the gang.

When Costa entered the business and the alarm went off, the junior members left him there. Having no loyalty to him, they just drove off, not really caring about what happened to him.

His gang had abandoned him. He couldn't believe it.

He was in tears. All that he'd lived for and built his life around was a façade.

I talked to him for about an hour and told him that the streets had changed; he had to realize that and change himself, get a job, and go "legit."

He screamed in my face, saying, "Look at me, bitch! Look at me! I'm gang tattoos, head to fuckin' toe—no one will fuckin' hire me! Do you think I haven't tried to get a fuckin' job?"

He then became sullen and said, "I'm in this shit for life. I made a mistake—a *huge* fuckin' mistake—but it's too fuckin' late to go back now."

I noticed that he had a set of scars on the back of his neck. They looked really nasty and deep, so I asked him about them.

He told me that he'd been stabbed in a gang fight in prison and was nearly killed.

Now he was shaking and crying at the reality of what his life had become.

This wasn't what he'd envisioned years earlier, not what he'd hoped for—and now he'd been abandoned and betrayed by his gang, despite the fact that he wore "St. Pauls Trece" tattoos all over his body.

He was booked into the jail that night, and I never saw him again.

He did the rest of his time and got out of prison.

He attended another St. Pauls 13 party when he got out, but at this one he was stabbed again in the back of the head.

This time, he died at the hands of one of his own gang's members.

He lived the reality of being a gang member.

There is no golden age of respect later in life, and you'll never be a respected street soldier; you simply die angry, early, and alone.

Unfortunately for the senior gang members, this was a common story.

I heard many variations of this same theme from the elder gang members I spoke to.

Not all died, but all weren't happy at the lack of respect that the younger generation had for them or the work that they'd done in the name of the gang.

This wasn't unique to a specific family cell of SP-13 either; it was across the board.

In the Ortiz family, "Bird" Ortiz told me this same thing.

In the Lucero family, it was "Bear" Lucero who told me this as well.

Juan and Felipe Gallegos also commented on this lack of respect by the peewees; it seemed that it spanned across the entire gang.

The old days of respecting the senior OG members were over; no one would listen to them or cared about what they thought.

The new breed of gang members lived for the moment.

They were only concerned about today, and they held no respect for anyone but their immediate circle of homies.

This was the reality of gang membership, and even that little bit of respect and loyalty was fleeting.

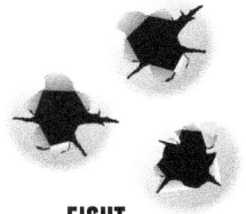

FAMILY REUNIONS

I FIRST MET BIRD ORTIZ in the 4000 block of Adams.

He'd just gotten out of federal prison for dealing drugs *(mostly cocaine)*, and he was at his brother Waldo's house, drinking beer and checking out the new motor that Waldo had just dropped into an old Chevy Impala.

While they were talking and getting re-acquainted, Bird saw the same guy who had ratted him out and sent him to prison.

The guy was walking down the street, so Bird confronted the snitch and they had words.

Bird pulled out a gun and shot at the guy, missing him but making his point that he wasn't happy about being ratted out to the cops.

I assisted the patrolman who'd been assigned the case, and we took Bird into custody.

I spoke Spanish and had overheard Bird asking his brother to take responsibility for the shooting so that he didn't have to go back to federal prison.

But Waldo refused to take the credit; no way was he doing time for his brother's mistakes.

While we sat there, Bird's mother came up and was yelling at him about being arrested already. She was really furious, and I had to get out and keep her away from the patrol car; she wanted to beat his ass big time.

I found out from her that Bird had three children she'd been raising while he'd been in prison. She'd hoped that he would get out, end his life of crime, and be a father, but with him being arrested again so soon, she knew that he'd be going back to prison and that she'd be forced to continue raising his children. She was *really* not happy about this.

I told her that she could bring the children to say goodbye to their father, but that was about all I could do for her.

She brought out two very young boys and a little girl to give Bird a hug goodbye.

He was crying and begging me to let him go, and he kept telling me that it was his brother that had shot at the guy—not him.

He said that he'd write a statement against his brother and "swear to it on a stack of Bibles."

I didn't tell him that I understood the conversation between him and his brother.

When the other officer investigating the shooting had the witness statements he needed and enough information, he came to the police station and took Ortiz to jail.

The next time I saw Bird was after I'd left the Gang Task Force and was working in the schools.

I'd been assigned to a school that had a mix of inner city kids and rich kids from well-to-do families. Both sets of kids had identical problems.

The inner city kids had parents who worked hard to survive, sometimes working two jobs over eighty hours a week; they were from broken homes and had poor parenting at home.

The rich kids had similar problems; their parents were rarely home, working eighty hours a week and making a lot of money—and they were never around to be parents for the kids either.

It was an eye-opening experience to see how similar the problems are between the really poor and the really rich.

One day, the principal called me into her office and explained that a guy had arrived fresh out of prison and demanded to see his children. He'd just been released and had come to the school with his parole officer's permission to see them.

She described him as very angry and extremely intense, and she wanted me to stand by while she called the school district administration for guidance.

I went to the office—and there was Bird Ortiz.

He'd grown considerably. He was heavily muscled and obviously still very much in the prison mindset.

I asked him to come to my office.

He asked why, saying that he wasn't going anywhere until he was able to see his children. We talked for a few moments, and he became more and more hostile.

I cut him off, saying, "If you wanna see your children, it's through me."

He said, "What the hell does that mean?"

I said, "That means if I say it doesn't happen, it won't happen—so you better start fuckin' workin' with me, Bird."

He was shocked that I knew his street name and who he was.

He asked how I knew him, and I told him we could talk in my office because it was more private there.

He agreed, and we went to my office and talked for several hours. I let him vent and tell me about how he'd lived in prison and missed his kids.

I explained that I was there when the last shooting had occurred and that we'd talked back them. He didn't remember me at all.

I told him that if I could, I'd get him to see his kids, but that he had to be patient.

He said he just "wanted to see his baby girl"..he kept repeating that over and over.

I could relate to that. I was estranged from my own daughter at the time, and I knew the hurt he felt.

I told him that I'd see what I could do about speeding up the process, but that he had to calm down and try to be less intense and angry.

The people in the school weren't street soldiers; they were civilians not familiar with the street—and they were terrified of him.

He agreed to try to calm down, and I left him in my office and checked in with the principal.

She said that they'd made the decision to allow him to see his kids and that each had been asked if they wanted to see him.

The boys had said "No," they didn't want to see him; their mother had done too much damage to the relationship that they had with their father, constantly badmouthing him to the point where they had no desire to see him.

Besides, they barely remembered him. I could relate to this also.

I told him that the boys refused to see him but that his daughter was on her way down.

He was clearly shaken up by this.

He said that his kids were all that kept him going in prison; he couldn't imagine why they wouldn't see him.

He was getting pissed off again, so I had to settle him down and told him that I'd walk his ass out of the school in handcuffs if he didn't calm down.

He still had his daughter on the way down, and at least that was a start.

I told him that he could see her in my office and have some privacy there, so he calmed down a bit—but he was still really anxious.

When his daughter walked in, he completely fell apart.

He started sobbing, then he grabbed her and started hugging and kissing her.

He was talking but making no sense at all, babbling nonsense. He then picked her up and held her in his arms like a baby and sobbed loud, gasping sobs.

She was just as emotional, crying "Daddy, Daddy."

I left them in the room alone for about an hour.

It was a very moving scene, not what you'd expect from a hardened federal prisoner just released from the joint.

Finally, they came out of my office and she went back to class.

He then came up to me, tears still in his eyes, and thanked me over and over, saying that he owed me one for that time alone with his daughter. He then left the school and went back to the halfway house.

I dealt with him many times over the next few years as he struggled to re-establish himself back into "normal" life.

His daughter and sons eventually did form a relationship with him, but they got into trouble a lot, and when I'd write cases on them he'd plead with me to try to keep them "out of the system."

He repeatedly asked that I "keep their jackets clean and free from paperwork," but I told him that that was his responsibility—not mine.

He couldn't understand how to be a parent.

He could lead gang members to survive in federal prison and on the street, but he had no idea how to parent his own children and keep them from following him into the penal system.

As he expected me to make exceptions for his kids that I wouldn't make, our relationship continued to be tense.

Finally, I grew tired of his complaining, and I told him that since he was an OG and had "**Street Creds**" he should be able to control his own kids.

He said that he couldn't and recounted the lack of respect for older gang members that I mentioned earlier; in response, I told him that he had to reach his kids as a father to his children—not as gang members.

He couldn't understand that; to him, there was no difference...that's how ingrained the lifestyle was in his mind and family.

The entire Ortiz family was deep in SP-13.

The boys had a cousin named NaNa, and both of her parents were also serving time in prison for dealing drugs. She was living with her grandfather, and he really hated her.

At thirteen, she was openly a lesbian, and he felt that was an affront to God and regularly beat her if he caught her engaged in any lesbian activity.

She was tough as hell and as much a leader in the new crop of peewee gang members coming up in the city as any male.

She also hated cops, and I was never really able to develop a relationship with her.

I did get her to talk to me eventually, though; she opened up a little bit after I arrested her grandfather for beating her up with a phone.

He'd caught her having sex with one of her girlfriends and beat her with the handset of an old style telephone, badly bruising up her face.

Eventually, she'd even play basketball with me on occasion. She was really likeable and tough.

Last I heard, she ran away from foster care, and I never heard from her again.

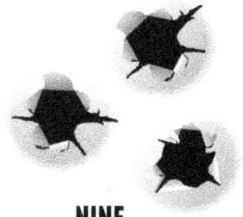

SNOOPY MEETS SNOOPY

MARK SOUTHWICK, AKA "SNOOPY", BELONGED to the 8 Ball Crips.

He was married to a sheriff deputy's daughter. They had a one-year-old son and were on their way to a friend's house to celebrate his first birthday.

When Southwick pulled into the apartment complex at 610 Redwood Ave, he said he immediately knew that it was a mistake.

He had to drive through a bunch of SP-13 gang members standing in the driveway of the apartment complex, and they started talking shit to him as he drove through the crowd.

Southwick said that he went to his friend's apartment to see if he was home. He was, and they talked for a few minutes.

They each decided that maybe that night wasn't a good night to have the birthday party since the SP-13 members were there at the complex, acting very aggressive, throwing up their hands, and challenging Southwick and his friend whenever they happened to look over.

Southwick said that he got into his car and told his wife to roll up the window.

He then told her to lock the door and that they were leaving the complex.

As he started to drive down the driveway to exit the complex, though, the SP-13 group split up, approximately half on each side of the driveway.

Southwick could tell that one guy in particular looked really angry, and this guy came up to the driver's side of the car and told him to roll down the window.

Southwick did, later saying that he did it to "avoid looking like a punk". He didn't want to appear to be afraid of the SP-13 set.

The angry guy asked Southwick what gang he claimed, and Southwick replied 8 Ball Crips.

The SP-13 gangster replied, "This is big time St. Pauls Trece, fool!" then pulled out a gun and shot Southwick point blank in the chest.

Southwick hit the gas and drove out as fast as he could.

After he pulled out of the area, he eventually pulled over and stopped.

He then had his wife drive because he was starting to pass out and go into shock.

She quickly drove him to the nearest hospital Emergency Room.

When he arrived at the Emergency Room, I received the call and went there to investigate.

I got the basic information from him about what had happened.

He thought that the shooter had been Pedro Lechuga; he said that he'd met Lechuga once before.

I told him that I knew who Lechuga was and that I'd go find him.

I then asked Southwick if he'd be willing to provide written statements and look at a photo lineup.

He said that he'd cooperate with the investigation, so I asked him to call me when he left the Emergency Room.

Amazingly, his injuries weren't critical or life-threatening. He'd been shot in the chest, but he was really lucky. The bullet had hit a rib and traveled up to the sternum. It stopped there, never entering the chest cavity or hitting vital internal organs. He was out of the Emergency Room in a few hours.

I hit the streets, looking for Lechuga.

I knew that he wasn't an SP-13 gang member; he claimed the "West Side Pirus" at the time.

I went back to the apartment complex and found no evidence of the shooting, nor did I find anyone that would admit to seeing anything.

I was left with no witnesses, and no one would cooperate.

The only information I could gather was from a woman who would talk to me briefly, only to tell me that the police department had abandoned them *(the occupants of the apartment complex)*. They'd called over and over again to report gang shootings, loud parties, drug dealers, and everything else you could imagine, and the cops would come and take reports and leave—doing nothing else.

She said, "You won't get any help here from any of us."

This was typical of the responses I received on most gang calls, so I had to prove to them that I meant to stay and deal with the shooting until I solved it, earning back the people's trust. It was a long, hard process, and it took a lot of time.

I checked the apartment complex and found no West Side Piru graffiti. There was absolutely none; however, I did find a lot of SP-13 graffiti.

I figured that Southwick must have been wrong about his identification of Lechuga as the shooter, but I had to prove that before I could move on to figuring out who the shooter was.

I went to Lechuga's house and contacted his family. They told me that he wasn't at home and that he was at a wedding of a client.

The family had a band that they all played in, and they'd been booked for the wedding.

So, I went to the wedding to confirm if Lechuga was there.

The wedding was being held in the Hampton Inn.

It was for a gang member that was SP14, a Nortaneos set—and it wasn't a friendly environment.

SP14 was a Hispanic gang that claimed red as their color. They were a very small and very quiet set.

There were some really hard-core gang members at that wedding, and they weren't happy to see me there at all.

But, I found Lechuga's parents and explained the situation, telling them that I'd be willing to let them continue playing in the band for the wedding as long as they'd give me their promise that they'd bring Pedro to the police station after the wedding. If they wouldn't agree to do that, then I'd have to take them out of the wedding.

They agreed to come to the station when the wedding was over; as a result, they had some very angry people at the wedding that they had to calm down.

The Nortaneos were very upset that the Lechuga family had told the police that they were at the wedding in the first place; needless to say, they were really pissed off.

Eventually, Pedro and his family arrived at the police station.

After much coaxing by me, they allowed him to give me a statement and take his photo for a lineup.

I then had a patrol unit run the photo lineup past Southwick, and he verified what I already knew: Pedro was *not* the suspect.

I advised the Sergeant, about this, and he told me that Southwick was duping me. He was sure that Southwick was lying and that he'd now know what Lechuga looked like and would go after him on his own.

I thought that was ridiculous and made no sense, but it wasn't our first disagreement, so I just ignored him.

I went back to the apartment complex night after night, trying to get someone, anyone, to talk to me.

Finally, I had a guy approach me and tell me that he knew who had done the shooting and that the guy lived in Smithtown.

The shooter claimed SP-13 and went by the nickname "Snoopy", but he thought his real name was Anthony.

I accepted his help and gave him my pager and cell phone numbers. I then worked the apartment complex nightly for two weeks, asking patrols to meet with me there.

I'd walk around the complex from all different approaches, trying to win back the people who lived in the area.

I handled any cases that came up while I was there, and eventually people started to talk to me and greeted me with smiles and waves.

One night, I got a call from the informant.

He called himself Tony, and he said that he was throwing a party for a bunch of the gang members who had been in the area that night and that Snoopy would be there if they showed up.

It had been two weeks since the shooting.

He said that Snoopy had stayed in Smithtown until things cooled off and had cut his hair, hoping to disguise himself.

Finally, that Saturday night he sent a message to my pager that Snoopy was there.

I arrived and had a patrol meet me there.

I briefed them on what we were going to do, then went up the back stairway and had patrol approach from the front.

The occupants of the party saw patrol arrive, but by that time I was already in place.

As patrol came up the front steps, Snoopy went out of the apartment and tried to go down the back steps; I met him there, blocking his escape.

I asked him who he was, and he claimed to be Xavier Lechuga.

Xavier was a minor gang member associated with SP-13. I'd met him once about a year earlier, talked to him, and knew that he had a really bad stutter.

This guy, though, had no stutter at all—so I knew he was lying.

Additionally, he had newly shaved hair.

So, I placed him into custody and put him in my car, then instructed the patrol unit to break up the party, acting like we'd been called out to a loud party.

The patrol unit did just that while I transported Snoopy to the police station.

It took me less than two hours to get him to confess.

I had a photo lineup made up with his picture in it, then sent it to Southwick with another patrol unit; he immediately picked out the suspect I had in custody.

I informed the suspect of that and told him that his only option was to be honest with me.

I told him that we *(the police, the judges, and the jails)* were sick of all the gang members coming into the city from other places. We were loyal to St. Pauls as well, and I understood his disgust at all the gangs coming into St. Pauls.

I asked him to help me. Of course, this was a ruse—but it worked.

He caved and told me the account that Southwick had recalled, except for one small detail: he said that after he'd shot Southwick in the chest while he sat in the driver's seat of the car, he reached back into the back seat and tried to fire one shot into the chest of their infant; saying he "wanted that fucking dirty kid dead with his poser father."

He said that the gun jammed, though, and he didn't know why.

I had him read the statement that he'd given me and correct any mistakes I may have made. *(I made mistakes on purpose so that he'd have to read it and fix them. It was a trick I learned from another detective; this technique made sure that the suspect could read and that they couldn't claim that the statement was forged.)*

I booked the suspect Anthony Mascarenas *(Snoopy, SP-13)* into jail.

He went to court and pleaded guilty to the shooting.

His mother claimed that he'd been forced to sign the statement, stating that he couldn't read at all; however, the corrections he made to the written statement proved that she was lying, and I advised his attorney of those facts.

Later, Southwick would tell me that his nickname for the 8 Ball Crips was also "Snoopy"; he thought that was a weird coincidence.

After I told him about the disclosure that Mascarenas had made about trying to kill his son, Southwick was really shaken up and started to withdraw from the gang life.

He sold his car and changed jobs, and he quit hanging out with all the 8 Ball gang members except for his closest friends.

This was the end of his active gang membership.

He didn't quit the set completely, but he did withdraw from the active gang life, parties, and fighting and drive-bys.

This was good for a period of time, but then his wife got bored.

She liked gang life, and she wanted it and the excitement that went with it.

They ended up divorcing, and she started dating another SP-13 member. This drove Southwick into a rage, but he still didn't go back to active gang life.

I later asked Southwick about how he came to be in 8 Ball and not any other set. He said that he'd wanted to join 8 Ball and liked the name and what he felt they stood for.

He and a few of his friends drove to Denver and met up with some 8 Ball members there.

When they asked to be jumped in *(to be made legitimate 8 Ball members)*, the set did jump them in, then Southwick and his friends brought 8 Ball back to St. Pauls.

I asked him how they met the 8 Ball members, and he said that they'd met them at a concert in Denver.

Later, he'd help me on cases that involved people he knew as long as they didn't require him to give up anyone in his set.

He gave me another set of eyes on several cases, which saved me a lot of time.

Anthony Mascarenas did end up in jail, then went on to prison.

I was told after he'd been there about a year he stabbed a guy and tried to kill him, extending his stay in prison for some time. He was only nineteen when I arrested him.

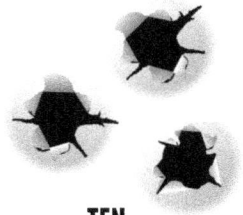

IT'S ALL ABOUT FAMILY

PEDRO LECHUGA WAS A WEST Side Piru.

He came from a family that had been in St. Pauls for generations and had associated themselves with SP-13. They claimed as a family to be members, or associates of St. Pauls 13.

One day, a few months after the Snoopy shooting case, they called me to report that Pedro had been beaten up badly at a party in west St. Pauls.

I talked to Pedro, and he wouldn't tell me what happened, only that he'd been at a party with some friends and that they jumped him.

I went to some of the guys that he hung out with and asked them what happened; from their response, it was obvious that they'd changed their opinion of him. They didn't speak highly of him, calling him a "punk" and a "bitch."

It took a while to figure out what had really happened, and I ended up going to his girlfriend—who now claimed that she was his *ex-girlfriend*.

She said that Pedro had been at the party and had been drunk.

He got into an argument with her and beat her up badly. She was really well-liked in the WSP set, and the guys in the set got pissed off, telling Lechuga to knock it off or face the consequences.

He told them to fuck off, that she was his girl and he'd beat her ass if he wanted to.

They told him again to stop, and he didn't, so they beat him up, making a point of ensuring that he got the message.

They beat his ass pretty good, and he was no longer welcome in WSP.

He was out on his own with no one covering his back.

I verified this story with some of the guys at the party without telling them where I'd heard it.

They just assumed that he'd told me, and they were even more upset that he'd told the cops what had happened.

I then told his parents what had happened and why, and they made a point out of telling him *(with me in the room)*, "You wanted to go with these guys. You said 'red was cool' and to give it a chance. They are *not* your family, Pedro—which is why they beat you up. You need to come back to the family."

A few months later, I heard that Pedro had been jumped in to St. Pauls 13; his family had wanted him out of the WSP and in with SP-13.

As an adult, I saw Lechuga.

He'd taken his family's advice and joined the "family gang".

Another generation of gang members was rolling down the assembly line.

This is a hard inheritance to break.

The wealthy families have their traditions: college at top tier schools like Harvard or Yale, membership at "exclusive" social clubs—all to keep a reputation among the elite.

The poor have them as well: gang membership, prison sentences, a "jacket" in the system—all to keep a reputation on the street.

It never ceased to amaze me the similarities between the two groups and their kids...neither group seemed happy to me.

TRUST NO BITCH

I WAS AT HOME ON my day off, playing basketball with the kids, when the phone rang.

I checked the Caller ID, and it was work calling again. I sighed and picked up the phone.

There was a guy in the hospital who had been stabbed at a party earlier that morning. He was a suspected gang member, and the circumstances made it seem gang related...so goes another day with my kids shot to hell.

I said goodbye to them and went to work.

After I arrived at the hospital, I spoke to the victim, who had just come to the ICU from the operating room; he'd been in the OR for several hours, having his abdomen literally pieced back together.

His name was Rene Ruiz, and I recognized him from working patrol.

He was really in a lot of pain, so as I tried to get a statement from him I was barely able to ask questions and get him to answer. It would be some time before he was out of the hospital, though, and I needed his statement to get on the case immediately.

He said that he'd been invited to a party in the basement of 2351 38th St.

He showed up and was talking to this girl who had invited him. He liked her a lot, and while they were talking he said that four other guys showed up. He didn't know them, but he could tell that they were SP Treces.

He was 7th Street Mafioso, but no one said anything to him, and he felt relatively safe for a while.

The four SP Trece guys left, and he stayed and talked to the girl and some other people at the party.

An hour or so went by, then the four guys returned.

They'd been drinking Tequila, and their mood had changed drastically.

People started to clear out of the party immediately, leaving only him and the girl who lived in the apartment.

He said he thought that the guys from the SP Treces had left the party as well, but he waited for a while to make sure they were gone.

What he didn't know was that they weren't gone at all; instead, they were waiting for him just outside the apartment.

When he finally did leave, he said these four big dudes immediately surrounded him.

He was only about 5'6" and maybe 145 pounds; the SP Treces—all four of them—were well over 250 pounds and strong.

They got in his face and started to push him around. He tried to run, but they had other ideas for him.

They beat him up a little bit, then each one grabbed an arm or a leg.

Then, while they spread him out on the ground, a fifth guy appeared out of nowhere and pulled out a knife, opening up Rene's jacket and shirt and telling him, "We're gonna carve your ass up for messin' with one of our bitches."

The fifth guy was Jose Costa.

He stuck the knife into Rene's abdomen and slowly started to cut, gutting him like a fucking fish—literally spilling out his intestines and internal organs while he screamed frantically for help.

The victim could do nothing but watch his stomach be cut slowly open by the drunk Costa.

The other four guys were huge, and they had him pinned while they, too, watched him being cut open.

When I later talked to the girl who had the party, she said that she heard him screaming but wouldn't open her door in fear of what would happen to her or her child. She claimed not to know who the suspects were and gave me a very vague statement.

I still believe that she set Rene up.

It was very common in the gang world for the women to invite dudes to their apartments or to parties, promising to "hang out" or set them up with some girl who had wanted to meet them.

The gangsters have a saying: "*Trust no Bitch.*"

It's for a reason; women can get you killed really quickly in the gang world.

I worked several stabbings and homicides that were obviously caused by women setting guys up from rival sets.

Anyway, I didn't have much to go on in his statement; Rene couldn't remember who had cut him up as he struggled to stay awake while we talked.

I went back to the office, and the Lieutenant in charge of the gang unit told me that I'd have to work with Det. Liptrap on the case.

The brass assumed that I was out of my league (*according to whom, I don't know*), so he said that Liptrap would be in the next morning and that I'd brief him and follow his lead.

I was pissed. I hated Liptrap.

He was well known on the force as a liar who took credit for others' work. He also didn't know shit about gangs.

I worked until the leads ran out, then went home.

The next day, I came in early to try to get somewhere on the case.

Rene was awake, so I went to talk to him at the hospital.

He said he was feeling better, and he did remember one name. He was able to recall that the name of the guy with the knife was Jose Costa.

He said that he'd known Costa for years, in high school, middle school, and from the neighborhoods they grew up in.

He was absolutely sure that Costa had been the one to open up his stomach so mercilessly.

I knew Costa as well.

I went back to the station and made up a photo lineup, then took it to Rene.

He picked out Costa with no hesitation; he couldn't identify who had held him down, but he knew for sure that Costa had cut him open.

I left the hospital and went to Costa's house, but no one was there, so I left and went back to the station to do some more background work on him.

As soon as I arrived, Det. Liptrap came up to me and said, "Hey bud, I hear that we're working together on a case. What can you tell me about it?"

He was smiling in that typical, passive aggressive, fucked-up slimy way he had, knowing I was going to be doing all the work and that he'd be taking all the credit; this was his typical method of operation.

I thought about it and made a decision right there.

I looked at him and said, "I can tell you that I don't need or want your fuckin' help, so go back to your side of the room and stay there."

The smile disappeared from his face instantly.

He was one of the Golden Boys; he could do nothing wrong in the eyes of the brass and wasn't accustomed to being treated this way.

Instantly pissed, he stormed off and got on the phone immediately (*probably calling my Lt.*).

I left the police station, thinking my time remaining on the Gang Task Force was now down to a few hours; Liptrap would want payback for not giving him his due respect.

I went back out to Costa's house, and this time I caught him at home.

I told him that I needed to talk to him and that I needed him to come to the station immediately.

He was watching his kids and didn't have a sitter, so I waited at his apartment until his wife got home.

It took about an hour for her to arrive, and I was there the whole time, pretending that nothing was wrong as I talked to him and his friends—but I was still on edge.

On the inside, I was thinking that they'd try to shoot me or stab me at any moment; however, on the outside I was laughing and joking with them.

I was really pissed about how they'd carved Rene up, and I didn't want him to have any way of setting up an alibi, so I stayed.

After listening to him tell his wife that everything was fine, I drove Costa to the station; six grueling hours later, I was finally able to get him to confess to the stabbing.

He started out admitting only to being a driver in the car that they used to drive to the party.

I kept at him, though, and he eventually caved in step-by-step, first admitting to having got out of the car when he heard screaming.

Later, he was in the stairway when the stabbing started. Finally, he was holding a knife and standing over Ruiz.

He admitted that he and four other guys had held Ruiz down and that he'd taken the knife and slowly slid it into his abdomen.

He said he liked the way it felt slicing Ruiz' abdomen open and watching the terror in his eyes.

He hated Ruiz and felt that he was less than human because he was 7th Street Mafioso, and not one of his homies.

For some reason, he felt like he'd go home after this confession, and he protested loudly when I told him that he was under arrest.

He got up and started to try to fight, telling me I was fucked up; I reminded him quickly that he didn't have his four fat friends with him and that I had no problem beating his ass for what he'd done, then booking him into jail.

He backed into a corner with his fists up, but he gave up after a very brief struggle.

He then whined and cried about not being able to see his kids, ultimately claiming that he'd confessed in order to take the blame for his homies.

"Billy bad ass" with a knife had disappeared; the real Costa had shown up. It was late, and I booked him into jail.

I had a note on my desk to see the Lt. in the morning at 8:00 am sharp. I usually came in at 1:00 pm, so I figured I was being sent back to patrol for not appropriately kissing Liptrap's ass earlier in the day.

When I came in the next day, the Lt. called me into his office.

He said that he was going to fire me from the Gang Task Force until he found out that I'd made the arrest; he didn't appreciate me talking to Liptrap the way I did.

I told him that I wasn't going to work with Liptrap ever—period! If that was a prerequisite to being in the task force, then he might as well kick me out now.

He stared at me with his one eye for a long time. *(He'd lost an eye in the Korean War, and it was unnerving to have him stare at you; he knew this and used it to his advantage.)*

Finally he said, "You're a cocky li'l fucker, aren't you? Liptrap can teach you a lot, but if you don't want to work with him, then fine. Get the hell out of my office!"

As I got up and began to leave, he said, "Good job on Costa."

I still had a lot of work to do on the case, and I spent the next few days tying up the loose ends.

I'd successfully made a statement: from that point on, Liptrap and I were sworn enemies—but I handled my own cases.

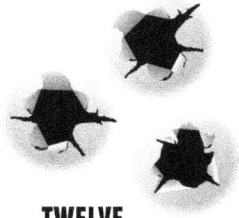

SPVG RAN THE CITY

BY THE TIME I ENTERED the Gang Task Force, SPVG had been deci-mated by the detectives who had been assigned at the time of the gang's rise on the street.

Jessie Afuvi headed SPVG at that time, and in my mind he was the single most charismatic and dangerous gang leader that the city of St. Pauls had ever seen. He was an excellent tactician, manipulator, and leader.

He'd lead by whatever method worked, using diversions, planning, and communications to successfully pull off several crimes, drive-bys, and armed robberies.

Under his leadership, the gang outmaneuvered the police almost nightly; he did this by using his brain and planning out everything that the gang did with military-like precision and tactics.

Eventually, though, Detectives Session and Rinker took SPVG apart and arrested Afuvi.

I was in patrol at the time, learning the ropes of battling the city's gangs.

I watched as the two detectives played gang members against each other, creating internal strife and external pressure on the gang.

They used rivals and women who hung on the gang members to get information on what was going on and who the players were, then went after them.

It was an education in full-scale urban warfare.

My part in SPVG began when the gang was at its highest point. From my perspective, they ran us ragged.

The patrolmen were running all over the city, putting out figurative fires that SPVG had lit.

It was night after night of shootings, drive-bys, gang fights, robberies, and aggravated assaults; they kept us busy trying to keep up.

They fought with one SP-13 family cell one night, then would drive-by another SP-13 house the next. It was intense street combat.

Eventually, Afuvi was caught and imprisoned, and leadership fell to a lesser leader, Leland Afuvi.

He'd been dealing drugs and running the streets since he was little; now he was an adult, and he tried to step up and fill Jessie Afuvi's shoes—but he couldn't.

He was a thug, but not nearly as smart or as driven as Jessie Afuvi.

I began working on him like I did the peewees in St. Pauls 13; I saw something in him that made me think he was vulnerable to the same kind of praise and kindness that the peewee bangers had been—and I was right.

I concentrated on him and him alone, paying special attention to him, praising his leadership and his ability to lead the gang.

Eventually, I was able to turn that and began to tell him that he was too smart for this street shit and should be thinking higher, towards school and a profession.

He ate that up, and in the space of about six weeks I had him to the point where he was ready to roll and give up the inside workings of SPVG.

He asked for a deal from the county attorney, giving him immunity for any crime that he'd done up to that date in exchange for information.

The county attorney agreed with a couple exceptions: they wouldn't grant immunity on any murders or rapes.

The deal was made, and one night I picked him up at home and brought him to the gang offices.

Before we left, I had to meet with his mother and convince her that I meant her son no harm.

I told her that the deal was real and that if her son wanted to start fresh, he could after that night.

She was in tears; she desperately wanted him out of the gang and drug life.

Their house had been subject to numerous drive-bys, and their cars had been vandalized over and over again.

The Afuvi family was right in the middle of the gang wars in St. Pauls.

Leland spilled it on the tactics and communications that the gang used, such as codes on pagers, checking in to make sure that everyone had made it back after a mission, and setting up alibis before ever committing crimes.

They used diversions to draw the police to one side of the city, then hit the other side after allowing for patrol response to the diversion.

They used pre-planned escape routes and relayed escape cars, meaning they switched cars along the way, both to and from the location that they attacked.

They'd use their girlfriends' cars, switching license plates—and they always had the women driving.

The police department thought of gang members as stupid and unable to function as an organized group; the reality was quite the opposite.

I learned a lot from this disclosure about how gang members worked together, as well as about their mentality.

I also learned how hard it was for members to leave the gang life.

About three weeks after the deal had been done with the county attorney, one of the central city cars got a report that a group of gang members had attacked a man in the middle of a gang neighborhood.

The man and some friends had been walking on the street late at night and had been jumped by another group of men who wanted to know who they claimed *(what gang)*.

According to the victims, they answered that they didn't claim anything.

The men then attacked them with knives and machetes, and one of the victim's arms was nearly severed; it hung by a few tendons and a small piece of meat, and the bones were completely detached after he'd been hit hard with a machete.

The patrol that was sent to the call put out a description of the suspect vehicle.

I had a reserve with me whom I'd let in on the whole deal with Leland Afuvi and his immunity.

He hated the idea and thought that it was a bad deal, and we were arguing that point when another unit picked up the suspect car in West St. Pauls.

I headed that way to help out.

The patrol car that had given chase to the suspects had ended up in front of a known SPVG gang member's house, and the occupants had bailed out and run, leaving the car running.

After the patrolman and one gang detective had stopped there, they decided not to chase them.

The detective was Mike Vetere.

I asked him where the suspects had gone, and he motioned toward the backyard of the house. I asked him if he was going to follow them, and he said, "Fuck that. I don't wanna get killed."

I replied, "To hell with that. *They* should fear *us*—not the other way around."

I then asked my reserve if he was up for the chase, and he said that he was.

We were off.

We tracked the occupants of the car down one-by-one, following their footprints in the fresh snow, until we ended up at a house.

The final set of footprints in the snow went in
 to the house and never came out.

We surrounded the house, and after brief negotiations with the owner—explaining that we could get a search warrant easily and search the entire house or he could let us in to get the suspect—he let us in.

There was Leland Afuvi, his immunity shot; he'd been involved in the machete attack, and now he was about to be charged for aggravated assault—or at least I thought so.

As it turned out, the detective assigned to the case *(Vetere again)* had never once had a case make it through court.

This case would be no different; he'd dick around with it, go through the motions, and make it look really fucking difficult until the interest in the case blew over.

I asked about the case over and over again, expecting to get a subpoena—but it never came.

Vetere had excellent evidence, but he could not *(or would not)* get the case to the level needed for court.

Afuvi was never charged, and I never let Vetere forget it.

I found out two years later that the victim in the case was, in fact, South Side 18th Street.

He'd told the gang detectives at the time that he claimed South Side 18th Street, but they were in denial about the gang being in St. Pauls.

They claimed that the guys who were on the street who claimed South Side 18th Street were liars and wannabes.

This would be a huge, huge mistake on the gang detectives' part; in a few short months, South Side 18th Street would be one of the major players in the city' gang culture.

For some time after that, the police department would continue to deny that South Side 18th Street had arrived in St. Pauls.

The next time I ran into Jessie Afuvi, he'd just been released from prison.

I was called into the Chief's office and given a picture of him and his release date. The Assistant Chief assigned to detectives then told me that "as soon as I had a case on Afuvi, I'd better make it stick."

He said that he "didn't want this motherfucker running us ragged again."

I agreed.

He was a formidable opponent, and it was now my turn to go head-to-head with Afuvi and hopefully get him convicted and off the street as soon as possible...I didn't have to wait long.

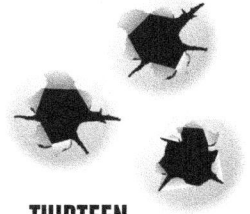

STREET RAP BEFORE FAMILY

JESSIE AFUVI HAD AN AMAZING reputation on the street. He'd worked hard to establish himself, and it meant everything to him.

When he initially got out of prison, he had to defend that reputation. He had a lot of people challenging him; like the St. Pauls 13 gang elders had learned, he found out that your reputation is challenged every day in the street. Gang life had changed; nothing was sacred in the gang world anymore.

As soon as Afuvi felt that he was forced into defending that reputation, I was given a case that involved him.

The complainant was Paul Ricos.

He was a member of WSP and had been in SPVG when Jessie Afuvi had rolled all of the smaller gangs in the city into SPVG a few years earlier.

He called to report that Jessie Afuvi had arrived at his house in West St. Pauls with his cousin Guy Dondo.

They'd come to his house after having a barbeque in the West St. Pauls Park.

According to Ricos, they said that he'd been talking shit about Jessie and that they wanted to "straighten things out with him."

Ricos went out of his house to talk with Jessie and Dondo.

He said that he told them that he hadn't been talking shit about Jessie and reminded him that they were cousins as well.

Jessie Afuvi then pulled a sawed off shotgun from his vehicle and grabbed Ricos' daughter, pointing the gun right at her head.

The discussion continued, with Jessie making it clear that he was out of prison now and back on the street—and he wouldn't tolerate anyone talking shit about him.

Ricos begged him not to harm his daughter, crying and pleading with him to leave her alone.

Jessie made sure that the entire family saw the incident and that he meant what he said.

He then told Ricos that if he heard anything else, he'd return and the girl would be harmed.

According to Ricos, Afuvi laughed at his concern for his daughter, then Afuvi and Dondo left the area.

I obtained statements from Ricos and his neighbors until I had enough information to get an arrest.

I then hit the streets and went out looking for Jessie Afuvi.

I went to his house, and his mother told me that he'd left in a brown Ford Crown Victoria with some friends to look for a job.

I hung around the area and eventually spotted the Crown Vic as it came across the 34th Street Bridge.

I stopped it and pulled Jessie Afuvi out of the car at gunpoint, then took him to the station and obtained a verbal statement from him.

We talked for several hours, and it was really interesting to see how much smarter he was than the usual suspects that I dealt with.

He was extremely bright and articulate; definitely a totally different animal.

He wouldn't admit to the incident, but he did say that he was struggling with how to stay out of trouble since being released from prison.

He said that since he'd been released, everyone was "talking all kinds of shit about him, knowing that he was on paper," hoping he'd be too afraid to confront anyone who talked bad about him.

He said that he had "not put in so much work to earn a reputation on the street to have it destroyed by the weak."

I told him I thought that he'd have to move from the area if he wanted to stay out of prison.

Reality was, he was now a target on the street, his reputation having made him one by both the gangs and the cops.

I told him that I'd been told that he was out of prison by the Assistant Chief and that I had orders to make any case with him stick.

He listened quietly but said nothing.

I then booked him into jail based on the statements I had from Ricos and other witnesses and waited for court.

When I finally did go to court, it was with charges of felony aggravated assault; I left with a conviction of misdemeanor assault.

Ricos refused to testify against Jessie Afuvi, neither would his family nor any of the other witnesses to the event; they all refused to talk in court, claiming they couldn't remember the incident and that they didn't write their statements—that I'd forged them.

I looked at Jessie Afuvi, and he smiled.

He'd told me that Ricos was a "bitch" and that he'd never testify against him in court.

After Jessie had threatened Ricos' daughter, I'd doubted that—but I was wrong.

I was barely able to get the conviction, but I did, and Jessie Afuvi was sent back to prison.

I had another case that Jessie Afuvi was named in, but I couldn't get anyone to provide a statement.

I did talk to some witnesses, and they all agreed that Afuvi was present and had participated. They wouldn't cooperate, though; they were too afraid of him.

The major crimes unit handled the case, and I was brought in as an assistant because it was considered gang-related.

SPVG was rumored to have had a coming home party for Jessie Afuvi. The party was in West St Pauls, and several people from outside the city were invited.

One girl was from Springdale and showed up to the party having no idea who she was partying with.

She started drinking and began talking shit to the party members, making racist remarks. She pissed off the SPVG guys' big time, so they coaxed her out of the house, then dragged her to a park near the railroad tracks.

Anonymous witnesses said that they could hear her screaming for help and that several men were repeatedly punching and kicking her as they took turns dragging her down the street towards the park. They repeatedly raped and beat her, then choked her to death.

They then dumped her body in the park in plain sight to make a statement: they would *not* tolerate disrespect.

This case was "solved" by major crimes; they were able to get JJ Jones to confess to being there and killing the girl.

In his confession, he claimed to have been the only person that had participated in the crime.

I had numerous people tell me that Jessie was there as well, and I approached major crimes with the information.

The unit wasn't interested, though; their idea was that they had Jones's arrest locked up and that to bring Jessie Afuvi in as well might impeach the arrest and conviction they already had.

I even had a "friend" of Jessie Afuvi tell me that she'd seen scratches on his chest and throat after the girl's murder and that she asked about them. He replied to her to forget she ever saw them—or she'd end up in the park as well.

She also wouldn't give me a statement about what she saw; she was too afraid.

Knowing about this case helped explain Ricos' fear of Jessie, as well as the witnesses' refusal to testify against him. If any of this is true, I still don't know; I was never able to prove it in court.

Afuvi was bigger than life on the street.

He'd built a reputation that made his life hell to live.

On the one hand, he was feared and respected by a lot of people; on the other hand, he was hated and blamed for a lot that he had no hand in.

This is another fact in gang life: your reputation can get you into trouble in many ways that you never anticipate.

HELL HATH NO FURY

WHILE I WAS IN THE Gang Task Force, I did have small breaks between the gang warfare.

During one of those breaks, one of the county attorneys called and asked me to investigate a claim by a 12-year-old girl who said that she'd been gang raped at an 18th Street gang party.

The girl, Amber Kilburn, was in the Juvenile Detention center called Pine Willow Bay. She'd been locked up for some minor charges and had been assigned a caseworker.

During one of the caseworker's many interviews, the girl broke down and began to talk about the incident.

The caseworker then called the county attorney, and the attorney asked me to look into it.

According to the attorney, the girl had identified known 18th Street gang members by their nicknames.

In addition, she also remembered the location where she'd been gang raped. It was an apartment complex, and she could describe it, but she couldn't remember the exact apartment number.

During the briefing the attorney said that the girl claimed to have been drugged and repeatedly gang raped by several men and boys at a party which was held in an apartment on 55th and Orchard.

I went to the apartment and checked the immediate area, looking for 18th Street gang graffiti; I found some graffiti, but not a lot.

I asked a couple women in the area if there had been any parties in the apartment complex in the past month or two, and they said yes, the men had had a party about a month earlier. One said that they had them every so often, but not frequently.

I advised the county attorney of what I'd learned, then went out to Pine Willow Bay to interview Amber Kilburn.

Initially, I thought that this would be a straight up interview; it turned out to be quite the opposite.

I had some difficulty just setting up the interview, having to call the attorney at home and get them to explain to the juvenile detention workers that I was there for the girl's benefit.

Juvenile Corrections is set up to protect the kids from the cops.

The people who work it usually take that idea to a whole other level and make it their mission in life to protect the kids; some even end up adopting the kids they run into.

After the prosecutor threatened to charge the workers with obstruction of justice, I was eventually granted access to a small interview room.

Kilburn was brought to the room after she'd eaten dinner, about twenty minutes later.

Initially, she started out acting like a little kid.

She was twelve at the time of the interview, and she acted like a normal 12-year-old kid: talking, acting nervous, and asking silly questions.

Interviewing techniques require that you set up the interview, watching the person you're interviewing, noting body language and eye contact, observing what's normal for them when they're relaxed and at ease; Kilburn wasn't relaxed and acting like a normal 12-year-old, though.

Every room in the facility was under camera surveillance, and the kids locked up there knew that; so, I had to talk quite a while to get Kilburn to let the façade drop.

There was no way the girl I was talking to would have been invited to an 18th Street gang party, much less actually attend.

Her body language eventually changed from a self-conscious 12-year-old to a slouching, much older streetwise female.

I then started to hit on the claims that she'd made, having her start from how she was invited to the party and by whom.

She claimed that she liked a "boy" and that he'd invited her to the party.

He hadn't told her that it was an 18th Street gang party; instead, he said that the party was just for some friends.

I asked her who the boy was, and she said he went by "Sleepy." She identified him by his gang name, not his real name, and this told me a lot about the "little girl" I was talking to. *(Everyone doesn't know gang names; in fact, the gang name is rarely known by anyone outside the gang culture. Most parents have no idea that their children have gang names and alter egos.)*

The 12-year-old girl was suddenly back, sitting up straight, playing with her hair, and smiling shyly.

I asked her to continue, and she outlined sneaking out of the house and going to the party with a girlfriend.

She said she was nervous about being at the party alone with "Sleepy," telling me how he'd coaxed her into a room and offered her a "blunt". *(She described a "blunt" using that term exactly.)*

I asked her what a blunt was, telling her that I'd never heard that term.

She laughed at me and said, "Really? Everyone knows what blunts are!"

She then laughed at my "stupidity" and started to relax.

The Juvenile Corrections workers had interrupted us several times by this point, telling me that I had limited time with the girl.

Finally, I had to remind them of the threat to be charged with obstruction of justice by the county attorney. I asked how their bosses would feel about them being charged and working there, alluding to the fact that their jobs were now at risk if they continued to interrupt.

Finally, they left us alone.

Surprisingly, Kilburn relaxed, and when I started to get into the details of the gang rape her body language changed.

It didn't change the way it should have, though; she became more relaxed, leaning forward and loosening up, rather than closing off and taking a more protected posture.

She made eye contact comfortably and kept her arms and legs open and relaxed.

She then recounted waking up on the bed with her legs high up in the air, saying that two men held them while two other men held her arms.

She said that a grown man *(she described him as maybe 40)* was raping her.

She said she was really out of it and looked around the room and saw that it was filled with men all chanting in Spanish, encouraging the rapist to "keep fucking her". *(Her words.)*

She said that she passed out, and then became conscious again several times.

Each time, a different guy was on top of her, and each time she heard the cheering and clapping by the onlookers.

She didn't know any of the men that she recalled raping her, so I asked about the claim by her caseworker that 18th Street gang members had raped her. *(I hadn't told her that I knew Sleepy and that he was 18th Street.)*

She said that when the men were done with their turn, the "boys" took theirs.

She described several 18th Street gang members by their gang names: Perico, Sleepy, Silent, Wicked, and Penguin.

She said they rolled her over and preferred to fuck her from behind.

While she was recounting this, her body language had changed drastically.

She was no longer leaning forward; instead, she started leaning back and making suggestive eye contact, tracing a line up her inner thighs with one finger nearly to her crotch while pulling down her T-shirt with the other hand.

Exposing her training bra, she looked at me without breaking eye contact, smiling and licking her lips.

The timid 12-year-old had disappeared. *(When interviewing, paying more attention to body language and the way something was said was always more important than the message that the person wished you to hear; this was a great example of why.)*

She went into great detail about each gang member and what he did to her.

I asked her what happened with Sleepy, and she started to describe how, when it was his turn to "rape" her *(her terms had changed again)*, he was reluctant.

She said that the men were laughing at him and telling him he was a pussy.

As she recalled this, she laughed as well, saying, "There I was on my knees, legs spread out, my ass in the air, pussy there for the taking—and his shit couldn't get hard!"

This was quite a change from the timid little girl that I'd met at the beginning of the interview.

I said nothing, simply staring at her as I watched her body language change and evolve.

I had her recount the story again, and the more she told it, the more streetwise she became.

Her language changed, her attitude changed, and by the last time she recalled the incident she described the alleged gang rape in almost pornographic terms.

She described men "nutting" inside her and forcing her to swallow their "jizz"; as I knew they monitored the interview, I wondered what the juvenile workers were thinking now.

I finally called her on the inconsistencies of the rape, and after about fifteen minutes of her calling me a piece of shit and a worthless cop and telling me I was covering for the 18th Street gang *(she also claimed over and over that we cops were covering up the crimes by 18th Street)*, she finally admitted that she'd made the gang rape up.

She told me that she'd been having sex for drugs since she was nine years old, claiming that she wasn't a prostitute because "whores did it for money" and she only "fucked for drugs."

I asked, "So you've been fucking for drugs since you were nine years old?"

She said, "Yes."

She didn't even show the slightest discomfort at the question or her admission.

She then said, "But I wouldn't fuck just anyone! They have to be 'fine,' and they have to have good drugs."

I asked her why she'd been so angry about Sleepy in the made-up rape story and recounted how she'd claimed he couldn't get hard.

She said that she liked him and wanted to have sex with him, but he refused because he knew she fucked for drugs.

She said he didn't want anything to do with her because, at one time or another, she'd fucked everyone in the gang for drugs; she was mad that he thought he was too good for her now.

She made the comment, "That limp dick don't know what he's missing out on!"

I said, "That's it? This whole story, all this time it was about him not wanting to have sex with you?"

She said, "Yes!"

That and he'd failed to pay her in drugs for a blowjob he'd finally let her give him.

She wanted her payment, and she wanted him to realize that he couldn't just use her and not pay what he owed her.

She was furious with me for seeing through the gang rape story and getting her to admit to the real story.

She called me a "lazy fuckin' cop" in one breath, then asked if I wanted to hook up when she got out of lock up in the next.

She was a mess.

After I terminated the interview and she was led back to her room, I began processing out of the facility.

The workers who were very cold and disrespectful to me earlier were now warm and friendly.

The senior supervisor even came out and said that he'd never seen anything like that.

He said the transformation that the girl went through from a scared, timid 12-year-old to a streetwise gangster bitch fucking for drugs was unbelievable.

He said that unless he'd seen it with his own eyes, he never would have believed it.

I smiled and said sadly that it was the nature of gangs. Hiding in plain sight from family and friends who weren't in the gang and having two distinct lives was normal for gang members.

I thanked him for letting me get to what really happened, then left the facility.

Kilburn was later released to foster care.

Meanwhile, her mother had been arrested for having sex with one of her underage boyfriends; sex crimes detectives later learned that she'd "turned out" her daughter at the age of nine to have sex for drugs, frequently telling her that she was better at sex than the girl and could steal her younger boyfriends whenever she wanted to.

As a result, they had an intense sexual competition for the little girl's boyfriends.

A few years later, I'd get a call from another juvenile case worker, who asked me to be a foster parent to Kilburn.

She said that Kilburn had specifically asked to be placed in my home because I was the only person that she'd never been able to lie to.

I refused the offer, and the caseworker became irate.

She said that I was a cop and that I needed to give back to the community and help this "poor little girl."

I told her that if she felt so strongly about it, *she* could take on Kilburn as a project; I refused to subject my kids to her.

She hung up on me.

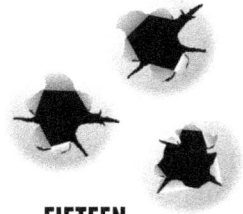

TRAVIS VICK AND PAT WALLACE

TRAVIS VICK (SANDMAN) AND PATRICK Wallace were both from smaller gangs that were rolled into SPVG under Afuvi.

Vick had earned the nickname "Sandman" for his ability to knock people out in a fistfight.

They were both very active under Afuvi, and both admitted to me that they feared and respected Afuvi immensely.

Wallace was a really talented cook and even earned a scholarship to a cooking school back east based on his talents; however, he refused the scholarship.

When I asked him why, he said that he was too afraid to be in another city, away from his "homies"; that's how ingrained the gang mentality was into him: he had a way out, and either could not or would not take it.

Both men ended up working in the kitchen of the local elite St. Pauls Golf and Country Club.

We in the gang unit and patrol laughed hard about this: the rich country club members were actually eating food prepared by Wallace and served by Travis "Sandman" Vick, both from SPVG.

The humor in this was way more than we could stand.

We often joked about our arrogant Chief sitting in the dining room of the country club with his family, eating and talking his usual shit about "his guys" and "his department," bragging about how he was personally making a difference in lowering crime in the city—all while eating food prepared by and served by the very gang members he was so determined to run out of the city.

This was a hilarious picture to us.

Pat was even featured in the local newspaper on a full front page of the Food section. The country club was very impressed with his abilities as a cook.

We laughed hard when we saw that.

Then came the final straw: pipe bombs were being found in the country club itself.

The management of the club was perplexed; how did pipe bombs get into the country club? Why would any one of their members bring them into the club to hide them?

They must have finally figured it out because Vick and Wallace were let go.

The elite people in the club lost their talented chef, and Vick and Wallace lost their hiding place for weapons and pipe bombs.

We sat in briefing afterward, wondering if anyone thought to ask the Chief how he'd missed the obvious fact that the cook and waiters were known members of one of the most notorious gangs in St. Pauls.

I know that this is really petty, but we liked the idea of his arrogant ass being served by these two SPVG gang members and him not even being aware of it.

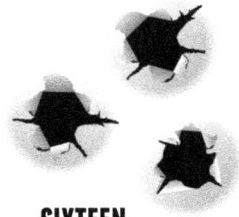

THE MAILMAN DELIVERED

I BECAME AWARE OF A small gang that had started to become very active in the city.

They were Crenshaw Varrio Lobos 13, and they'd arrived in the city as a small family group.

The Romero family had moved into the city, and several extended family members had arrived with them. There weren't a lot of them, maybe twelve members deep, and they aligned themselves with West Side 18th Street, which at the time was the more violent of the two 18th Street subsets in St. Pauls.

CVL13 was very skilled in shooting people and drive-bys, substantially better at it than any other gang in the city.

I was determined never to let another gang enter the city unchallenged like 18th Street had a few years earlier, so I made an effort to meet and talk to as many of them as I could.

I asked patrol units to contact me if they had any contacts with them, and I took photos of them every chance I got.

I also recorded license plates and car descriptions of anyone that they associated with.

I'd learned from the SPVG interviews and experience with other gang members that associates' cars were often used in drive-bys, frequently without the owners knowing what was going on.

The bangers would borrow the car to make a "quick run to the store," then go out and do a shooting, returning the car when they were done.

I started building an intelligence file on the gang, trying to stay ahead of the curve on their activities.

I also teamed up with a juvenile probation officer and began to accompany him on home visits with any West Side 18th Street gang members that associated with the CVL13 set.

I wanted to learn as much about them, their associates, and how they were structured as I could. They became part of my main focus for several months.

I visited one West Side 18th Street gang member with the juvenile probation officer who he said was one of the single most serious gang members he monitored.

The juvenile was nicknamed "Smoker," and the probation officer introduced me to him and his family.

As a result, I was able to see how he lived, his room, and his interaction with his family and their relationships.

This was really helpful later that summer.

One day, I came to work and received a case that detailed a shooting that had occurred in the 4300 block of Lincoln Ave.

A car had pulled up, and the occupants had called over a 14-year-old kid who was standing in the front yard.

There were three occupants in the car, and they made small talk with the kid, then asked him what gang he claimed.

The victim's name was Randy Choose.

He stated in the case that he claimed no gang affiliation and that the back seat passenger had yelled some gang name at him and the front seat passenger pointed a gun at him.

He said that he ran and that the guy with the gun shot at him repeatedly, finally hitting him in the ass as he approached his parents' car in the driveway.

He hid behind the car as the suspects drove off.

I went to interview Randy, and he said that he didn't know who the suspects were; he'd never seen them before and had no idea why they'd shoot at him.

I had no leads and no ideas of who the suspects could be.

The car they were driving was a red two-door, and Randy didn't get the vehicle's license plates; he wasn't much help.

I searched the neighborhood for witnesses of the shooting and found none. I had no leads, and the case was dead in the water.

A few days later, the gang secretary handed me some faxes that she'd received from the prison in the northern part of the state.

They detailed different gang activities in the city and had been sent to an inmate who had been a resident of St. Pauls, providing an inside look into the accounts of this particular gang member and what he told his friend in prison.

I had the secretary ask the prison to send me anything that was gang-related as soon as they got it, and they agreed to send whatever came their way.

A couple days later, they sent another batch of faxes.

One of the letters detailed an account of a shooting that had recently happened, talking about how the guy writing it went out hunting "Chochas" *(18th Street slang for St. Pauls 13)* with "Oso" and "Joker."

They drove several streets and finally located a dude in his front yard.

They pulled up to his house and called him over to the car, then asked him who he claimed because they wanted to make sure that he wasn't 18th Street; they didn't want to shoot an 18th Street gang member since they were aligned with them.

He said that they really didn't like hanging with the 18th Street gang members, but since they were such a small set, that was their only back up in the city.

The letter said that the kid told them he was "big time St. Pauls 13" and that Joker then came out of the back seat and pointed a gun at the kid.

The letter said that Joker told him, "This is Crenshaw Varrio Lobos Trece, bitch" and that he *(Joseph)* and Joker started shooting.

He said the kid ran and that they kept shooting until the guns ran out of ammo.

He said they then drove off, laughing and calling the kid a pussy for running.

He went on to say in the letter that he wasn't sure if they hit the kid or not and that he watched the paper for the next few days to see if the shooting had been reported.

He said that it was reported that they hit the kid in the ass and that the police had no leads, laughing about that and telling his friend in prison that the cops would never catch them because they were new and no one knew them in the city.

He said that he was pissed that they didn't kill the kid, only hitting him in the ass.

He then said that they'd have to practice shooting so that they'd be better at hitting their targets.

The letter was signed "Alrato", then "Joseph", and it had no return address.

This was an amazing look into the mindset of the gang member.

From an intelligence-gathering point of view, it was unprecedented in the police department; no one had ever had this kind of intelligence on gangs before.

The key with intelligence, however, was to make it usable.

Intel for the sake of intel was worthless; I had to find a way to make this into a conviction.

The case resembled my unsolved drive-by case enough that I went to talk to Randy Choose again.

He denied being St. Pauls 13, and he said that he couldn't recall what the shooter had said to him about what gang he claimed; he said he was too frightened to remember much.

I asked him if he could identify the suspects if I showed him a picture of them, and he said he couldn't.

Meanwhile, his parents were getting pissed off that I hadn't solved the case, and they wanted to know what I was doing.

I told them that I was working on it but that I couldn't make arrests out of thin air; I needed their son's cooperation.

They said that he'd done enough and that they would do no more to help me.

They then said that it was well known on the street that the "Gang Task Force" was in the 18th Street gang's pockets and that no one could get a case against them into court.

This told me a lot about the family.

They were obviously very deep into St. Pauls 13, not realizing that their statements gave that away.

It also showed me that I had a lot more work to do to overcome the reputation of the Gang Task Force.

I told the father that he was opening his family up for more shootings by not cooperating, but he just said that they would "take care of their own."

I left the house, pissed off.

I had a pretty good idea of who had done the shooting, but I only had uncooperative witnesses and a letter written by some guy I didn't know, detailing what had happened; I still had a long way to go.

I went back to the office and wrote up what had happened thus far, then added it to the case file.

I then learned that I had some more faxes from the prison waiting for me.

The same guy, Joseph, had written another letter detailing a rape that he'd committed on the boulevard.

He'd been driving a car that he borrowed and picked up a girl on the boulevard.

He then took her to a park and started making out with her.

He said that he started to take off her pants and she told him that she didn't want to have sex with him.

He said he told her that she knew what they were there for and that she wanted to fuck way too much to back down now, then forced her pants down and raped her on a picnic table in the park on 37th Street just above Washington.

He said that she was screaming for help but that no one came, bragging about how hard his dick was from her fighting with him and that she cried out when he came inside of her.

He detailed how he loved that she screamed for help and that he just kept raping her, saying that he liked how it felt and planned on trying to see how many more bitches he could rape on that table during the summer.

From that point on, I made this guy a target.

No rapes had been reported, and I had no victim, but with this fucked up letter he'd gone straight to the top of my "to do" list.

His name was Joseph Lucero.

He'd written a return address on the letter and signed it "Alrato", then his name.

I put his name out in patrol briefing that I wanted to be notified of any contact that any unit had with him.

I had his name and an address, but I still couldn't tie him to the drive-by on Randy Chase with anything but his letter; I was getting closer, though.

I continued to monitor Joseph, getting frequent calls to meet him from patrol units that contacted him.

I had a case in the 3500 block of Madison that he'd been involved in.

Several witnesses had reported that a car had driven past an apartment house on the east side of the street and that the occupants of it had yelled at a guy who was sitting in the front porch area of the house.

The guy had exchanged insults with them, then they started to shoot at each other.

The car then drove away.

Witnesses later identified the occupant of the apartment building as Joseph Lucero.

I went to the scene.

Patrol had enough information to make the arrest on Joseph, and I assisted by them by taking statements from the witnesses.

From that point on, we started having a lot of contact with CVL 13.

From the letters faxed to me by the prison, I knew that the leader was known by the nickname "Oso."

The main nucleus of members was Oso, Cisco, Joker, Chucas, and Joseph.

They hung out with West Side 18th Street gang members Silent, Smoker, Speedy, Bomba, and Wicked.

Patrol had several reports at Oso's house on 2251 Cottonwood of parties and shots being fired.

They'd responded to the house and asked for permission to search for weapons; Oso gave it to them, and they found none.

They then had harsh words with the occupants but no probable cause to make an arrest, so the cases were forwarded to me.

Two days later, Joseph wrote to his friend in prison, detailing how they'd hidden the guns and the stupid cops couldn't find them.

He bragged about how easy it was to get away with shooting in the city and that the local cops were nowhere near as smart as the cops in California.

He also sent pics of the people at the party, and now I had nicknames and pics to tie to the names.

Very few people were at the party, and patrol had taken names on all of them; by process of elimination, I had them all figured out except one: I couldn't find out who "Cisco" was.

I still didn't have probable cause for an arrest, but I was building a case against the entire set.

The next day, I was reading a huge pile of faxes about some other gangs in the city that were communicating with inmates.

The secretary of our task force told me that Detective Clark had a shooting that he'd closed without an arrest.

He had a habit of pissing off the victims in his cases by blaming them for the shooting, a tactic he'd learned from Vetere; they'd been pretty good friends and had worked together on cases.

This enabled the officer to "exceptionally clear" the case and was looked on by the brass as a legitimate closure of it; they felt it wasn't our fault if the victim wouldn't cooperate, particularly in gang cases.

She handed me the case and another fax, then said, "I held this one for you. You're the only one who may be able to do something with it; no one else cares."

I read the case, which detailed a shooting that had occurred in the 5500 block of Grant.

The case reported that Randy Choose *(again)*, his cousin Paulo Lumina, and their grandfather had been having a barbeque in the front yard of the grandfather's house.

A car had driven past with three occupants, went up about a block, then flipped a bitch *(made a U-turn)*.

As the car pulled up, the passenger window rolled down, and the passenger held out a handgun and started firing at the three guys in the front yard.

They ran for the house, barely missed by several of the bullets.

Inside the house were several younger children watching television; the bullets narrowly missed them as well. It was really lucky that no one had been hit.

The faxed letter was an almost identical account of the shooting, only it wasn't an eyewitness account by Joseph. He retold it to his friend in prison but said he hadn't been there, instead claiming that "Smoker" and "Bomba" from West Side 18th Street had done the shooting.

I called the Sergeant in charge of the gang unit at the time and told him that I had information on another detective's case.

He'd closed that case "exceptionally," and I wanted to take a crack at it.

The Sergeant wasn't happy that it was Clark's case; they were close friends. He thought it over, and then gave me the OK to pursue the case.

I went to the house on 55th and Grant and talked to the grandfather.

He was really angry, saying that he was never going to cooperate with the police department on anything.

He'd called the police asking for help, then had some "asshole detective" blame him for the shooting.

He said we were all incompetent assholes and that he had ways to deal with it himself.

I argued with him for at least an hour, but he wouldn't budge, refusing to cooperate.

I left a card with him and told him that I knew who had done the shootings, as well as the shooting of his grandson, Randy Choose, a couple weeks before.

I could get the arrests of the guys, who did the shootings and lock them up, but I needed the family's help; without it, I couldn't get convictions. He just had to trust me.

He still refused to cooperate, saying that he had connections and would take care of the shooter himself.

He'd taken his grandchildren out of the city and had them live with their uncle Vince; he said they'd be safe with him.

I disagreed, but he said that I didn't know Vince; he had a good name in "the joint" and on the street, and he was respected. No one would mess with him.

I then told him to ask Vince if he'd allow me to talk to the grandchildren to see if they could identify the shooters and ask him to convince the family to cooperate with me.

I knew who "Vince" was; he went by the nickname "Shady," and he was one of the original Ochoa brothers who were rumored to be the leaders in St. Pauls 13.

I told the grandfather that I wouldn't let this go and that one way or another I'd try to get these guys arrested for shooting at his grandkids—with or without his help.

I didn't know it at the time, but his wife was watching our argument from inside the house, which would later prove crucial to the case.

I left the residence, pissed off; it seemed like I was always fighting an uphill battle in gangs.

That night, Smoker had a drive-by done on his house.

He lived about two blocks away from the 5500 block of Grant.

There was one round shot through the front door; no witnesses, no vehicles seen leaving the area. Most likely, the shooter was on foot.

With only one shot, no car seen leaving in the area, and nothing yelled out about any gangs, it wasn't a typical gang shooting.

I think the grandfather believed he knew exactly who was in the car shooting at his house—and the grandfather had sent a message himself.

Fortunately for me and a lot of St. Pauls 13 gang members, though, the grandmother had different plans.

I called the county attorney who had handled my gang cases and set up a meeting, where I laid out what I'd collected in the CVL13 set.

Side-by-side, the faxes and the police reports detailed cases we had on record of the two shootings and the searching of Oso's house.

I explained the nicknames of the people listed in the faxes and who they related to, as well as the fact that there was one person I didn't have identified, named "Cisco."

It was a very complicated case, and it took a lot of explaining, and then re-explaining.

Eventually, once the attorney understood the cases, I told him that I wanted to try to pick up the entire set in one shot. I had to put a stop to this immediately; this was open gang warfare on the streets, and it was out of control.

I asked the attorney if I had enough to make an arrest, and he said that I did have enough for probable cause, but not conviction; I'd have to get more from the families to convict.

They also weren't sure about the admissibility of the faxed letters, but they seemed legally safe for court use.

I decided to go for it.

I called the Sergeant and explained my plan to try to locate the entire set and take them down in one arrest.

As we were talking, Detectives Tony Gamboni and Clark called me and told me that they'd just been dispatched to another shooting, this time at 4400 Quincy.

The victims were St. Pauls 13 members, and they'd been chased in their car by another car, a red two-door.

They'd wrecked their car trying to get away, and they said that the passenger of the car had gotten out and shot at them several times, narrowly missing their heads as they tried to get away.

They recognized the shooter as Joker.

They knew him from school; he attended the same high school as they did.

I knew Joker was from CVL13, so I told Gamboni to get statements and that I'd be out to help him as soon as I could.

I then updated the county attorney on this latest case and left, telling them that I'd call and let them know what we did.

I met the other gang detectives back at the station and told them what I planned to do.

After we briefed, we set out in the city, looking for the CVL13 set— but they were nowhere to be found.

It was a Friday night, the warmest night of the year so far; I remember that the radio station I listened to said just that.

An hour later, I met back up with Gamboni and Clark, and we decided to set up static positions in the city to try to locate the CVL 13 set.

Each of us took up a position on one of the main roads and waited; about two hours later, I saw a car with Joseph Lucero from CVL13 drive past me.

I was in an unmarked car, and they didn't see me.

I called out to the rest of the units and let them know where I was, then informed dispatch that I was trailing a car that had suspects in several drive-bys.

I waited for back up, but none came; so, I followed the car for several blocks, then finally pulled out the "kojack" single light I had for the car and initiated the stop.

I approached the car with my gun drawn and made it clear to the occupants of the car that if anyone moved, I'd start shooting.

I then told them all to put their hands on the roof of the car and keep them there.

The driver was Oso, and the front seat passenger was Joseph.

Joker was in the back seat, along with Smoker.

I made sure that I could see their hands and that they saw that my gun was out and pointed at them.

I saw that they were all wearing gloves and ponchos, and I asked them why. They said that they were cold *(in spite of it being the warmest day of the year)*.

I understood immediately that they were planning to do more drive-bys.

They were out hunting SP-13 gang members, and the ponchos hid their clothing and the gloves defeated the "gunshot residue" tests we did at the time.

They started talking a lot of shit to me, trying to fuck with me and get me flustered; I ignored that tactic and just made sure I could see all their hands and that no one caught me slipping.

I knew from their reactions that I had them by the balls this time; the newest gang in the city wouldn't slip past me like 18th Street had done to the detectives before me.

Finally, back up arrived and I removed them from the car one by one.

I took Joseph to my car first, and then left the scene to be processed by the other units.

We recovered three guns from the car and ended up taking almost all the occupants to the station for questioning.

I'm sure that we prevented them from doing even more drive-bys that night.

I interviewed Joseph for hours before he confessed to being the shooter in the Randy Choose case.

I told him that I'd been watching him for some time and that I knew everything he'd been doing in the city.

I outlined all the stories that I'd read in the letters that he'd sent to the prison, and when I was done I explained to him that he was new to the city and had no idea who I knew and who had been talking to me.

He was furious and said that when he found out who the snitches were that ratted him out, he'd kill them.

After talking for over six hours, he gave me a full written confession.

I then came out from that interview and prepared to interview Joker.

We'd briefed that we would each close our cases and interview *all* the suspects we had, rotating until we were all done; no one was to be booked or arrested until we were all done—but that hadn't happened.

Det. Clark had interviewed Joker, and when he confessed to the case that Clark had *(the shooting earlier in the day),* he took him straight to lockup.

He didn't let me know, and he didn't ask if I needed to see him; instead, he did everything he could to prevent me from interviewing Joker.

I was really pissed, but it was too late that night to do much about it. He was locked up, and I'd need parental consent or at least a guardian's permission to interview him.

I was pretty devastated by this; it was the most blatant in-your-face attempt to sabotage a case I'd ever encountered.

I continued on and booked Joseph into jail for the shooting.

I also interviewed him about the cases that had happened earlier, and he confessed to shooting at the suspects in front of his apartment about a month earlier.

Smoker had also been released before I could talk to him; it was done accidentally by a patrol unit at the scene of the stop on 3400 Adams.

I was really demoralized by these events.

It had taken a lot of work to get all the information together to make these arrests possible, and I hadn't expected to be so obviously back-stabbed by another detective.

I returned to work the next night and went to Smoker's house.

I'd met his parents several times with his parole officer and had established a pretty good relationship with them.

I told them I needed to see him, and they agreed to let me talk to him.

I then took him to the police station and told him that I'd arrested Joker *(a lie)* and Joseph as well.

I had enough to arrest him for the shooting at 5500 Grant on Randy Choose, Paulo Lumina, and their grandfather, and his only hope was to confess and admit what he had done; that was the only way the judge would consider giving him any kind of a break.

Of course, this was a bluff; I had nothing tying him to the shooting except the rough description of the suspect vehicle, which matched his father's car, as well as the faxed account from Joseph of the shooting.

Smoker felt guilty about being left out of the arrests and not being locked up like his friends, and I used that against him; in one hour, I had a complete confession.

He wouldn't tell me who the other person was who was with him when he did the shootings; he claimed that he was alone.

I knew from the letter that had been sent to the prison, though, that the other person was "Bomba" from West Side 18th Street—but I couldn't find him.

I went to his house, and the family claimed not to know where he'd been for several months. They said that he'd gone to Mexico and hadn't returned.

I arrested Smoker and placed him into Pine Willow Bay Detention for the shootings.

I then told his father what had happened and why his house had been shot at.

He didn't say much except that his son had disgraced the family, then closed the door to their house.

I left, then went to Randy Choose's grandfather's house and told him that I'd arrested all the shooters in every single incident that had occurred to his family.

I told him that the suspects had done more shootings and had nearly killed two other kids the day before; they were getting ready to shoot more people, but we'd pulled them over on the streets and they'd been stopped.

I again asked him for his family's help.

I'd done everything I'd promised, and they were all locked up; now it was up to him and the family to cooperate with me. If they didn't, there was a very real possibility that the shooters would get out of jail.

He listened but didn't say a word, instead just glaring at me.

He then closed the door on me, and I left.

When I returned to work a few days later, Randy Choose and his grandmother were waiting for me at the police station.

His grandmother wanted to talk to me alone.

She told me that she'd been listening to what I'd told her husband, and she wanted me to guarantee that I'd made the arrests of the suspects that I'd told him about.

I showed her the cases and the arrest documents, along with the confessions.

She then showed them to Randy and told him to cooperate.

He was hesitant at first, but he eventually provided me with a statement and a positive identification of Joseph from a photo lineup.

She left, returning a short time later with Paulo Lumina and her husband.

They both provided me with statements, and her husband *(the grandfather I'd been talking with)* apologized.

He said that he appreciated what I'd done and that Vince *(the uncle with the great reputation on the street)* had told them all to cooperate with me.

I was quite surprised by this statement.

I went to court on all of the cases.

Joseph pled guilty and went straight to prison; he was eighteen years old.

He was straight up about what he'd done and was adamant about finding out whom I'd talked to that had snitched on him; he made it clear that he intended to kill the snitch.

It was pretty funny to me that he was the snitch; the letters that he'd sent to his friend in prison had sealed his own fate...I don't know if he ever found that out.

When I went to court on Joker, it was a real eye-opener for the county attorney.

Det. Gamboni had been able to get him to confess to the case that I'd started.

He'd been called to testify in Juvenile Court, and he was sworn in and took the stand.

He was then asked by the county attorney assigned to the case a few simple, basic questions to establish probable cause for the arrest.

He'd taken a gun from Joker in the traffic stop that I initiated at 3400 Adams; it was a *six-shot revolver*.

The county attorney then asked Gamboni how many rounds he'd recovered from the gun.

He replied, "Seven," then thought for a moment and changed his testimony to "Five."

The attorney dropped that line of questioning and asked him if he recognized the case number on the court docs as an SP police department case.

He replied that he didn't and also said that he had no idea what the numbers were.

He was losing the case through his incompetence *(or maybe on purpose? I never found out)*, and the county attorney was both furious and amazed.

He came to the desk where I was seated and whispered, "I don't fuckin' believe this idiot! I'm gonna have to call you to the stand to save the case."

He then did just that, telling me beforehand that "you have to salvage this case, or we'll lose it."

I testified and cleared up the confusion in the 5/6/7 shot revolver. I also identified the case number as one of ours.

Eventually, Joker was certified as an adult and sent to prison at fifteen years of age.

He had an extensive record that included aggravated rape and aggravated assault, in addition to the drive-bys and attempted homicides.

Smoker was also certified as an adult and sent to prison. He was only seventeen years old.

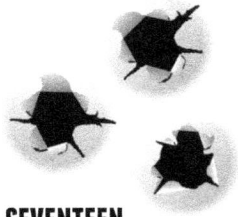

SCARECROW

THE WORD WAS OUT ON the street that CVL13 and West Side 18th Street were planning to retaliate for the arrests of their gang members.

I didn't know how serious the threats were, but I guessed at least one of my co-workers took them pretty seriously.

I was in front of the "Arcade Centre," a game arcade that used to be at the corner of 37th and Reynolds, talking to some 18th Street gang bangers; the business owner had asked that we make frequent stops at the arcade to keep problems with the gang members to a minimum.

I was talking to a group of about fifteen gang members with Det. Gamboni, who had been in the unit for about four months at the time.

I had my back to Tony and was talking to a kid—when suddenly the whole group started to laugh and point behind me.

I was surprised; the gang members rarely laughed at anything that wasn't dark humor.

When I turned around, I saw Tony hiding behind a car; he had ducked down behind my car and was hiding, scared and shaking.

I asked him what the hell he was doing, and he said that a red two-door had just slowed down across the street and he thought that the CVL13 gang was doing a drive-by on me to kill me for the arrests of their members.

He said all this out loud, so all the peewee 18th Street gang members heard him.

They all looked at each other, then at me, then rolled their eyes and started to whisper that he was a "bitch" and "what a fucking pussy."

I looked at the car he referred to and noticed that it was similar to the CVL13 car that had been used in several drive-bys.

"So when were you gonna tell me that they might be trying to shoot me?" I asked.

He didn't reply; instead, he just tried to ignore me while he got up from behind the car, then started trying to talk to the laughing gang members again.

They would have nothing to do with him, though; his true colors were now exposed.

I was pissed off as well.

Not only could he *not* count how many bullets were in a six-shot revolver, but now I discovered that he'd leave me out in the open without even a verbal warning that I might be getting ambushed.

I was done working with him.

I never let him ride with me again, and from that point on the gang members called him "Scarecrow."

CEASE FIRE

SHORTLY AFTER JOKER WAS CONVICTED, Oso was hanging outside his house, drinking.

He'd been pretty upset by the conviction of his nephew, Joseph Lucero, and his brother-in-law, Joker. He was alone now with only a few members of CVL13 left in the city—and they weren't the hardcore members.

I was monitoring him closely, checking on his residence daily in the hopes of catching him doing something that I could arrest him for.

I had several letters faxed to me by the prison that had identified him as the driver in numerous drive-bys, but they weren't enough to get him convicted in court.

I'd done my best to paint him as a possible snitch to the members that I'd arrested, trying to destabilize the group with doubts about who they could trust.

This was a regular practice for me: make an arrest and allude to the information coming from within the gang, sowing the seeds of mistrust.

With each arrest, I tried to create as much internal damage as I possibly could.

Psychological warfare was as critical to my success as actual street combat—not to mention winning cases in court.

Anyway, on this particular day Oso was outside, brooding while drinking and sitting in a lawn chair.

His daughter, wife, and several family members were outside with him as well.

I'd stopped by several times to check on him, and he was getting drunker each time I came by.

I talked to the family and listened to their apologies for the arrested family members' behavior; they apologized over and over again, but they had a very angry edge to their apologies.

I listened, hoping to learn more about the gang, as well as the relationships within the family; maybe I could use this against them later.

The gang had been dealt a serious blow with the arrests, but they'd want to recover, and I felt I had to prepare for their next move.

Like I said, I made several trips to Oso's house that day, the last one of which would be the most noteworthy; it would prove to be a severe test of my ability to rise to the gang members' level on the street.

At about 2 am, I was on my way home when I got that creepy feeling again.

I've mentioned it several times in *CurbChek*, as well as this story.

Something was about to happen—something really fucked up—and I had a very overwhelming, intense feeling that I should stop by one more time.

So, I turned around and drove back in to the city.

Twenty minutes later, I arrived at Oso's house.

The majority of his family had left, and all that remained were his wife and daughter in the front yard.

Oso had sobered up a bit, but he was surly as ever.

He made some half-serious, half-joking comments about shooting me in my car in front of his house.

I laughed loudly and replied that he'd be dead before he took his first shot, telling him that I already had my gun out and pointed at him through the door of my car.

He said, "Bullshit, ESE!"

I told him I wasn't like the other cops; I'd kill his ass in a second, but I'd talk to him as well.

He carefully walked up to the car, looked in—and saw my gun pointed straight at him.

He then looked at me, smiled, and said, "Damn, Ese—you're fuckin' serious!"

He laughed and told his wife that I had my gun pointed at him.

She made no comment; just watched us, keeping their daughter close to her.

Oso looked at me for a long time and didn't say a word, the tension continuing to build between us.

Finally, he started talking quietly about being worried about Joker and how he'd be in prison, wondering if he'd be OK. He had a lot of heart, but at fifteen he was very small.

He asked me if I thought he'd be OK, and I replied that I didn't know. I knew nothing about what prison was really like; I was on the outside looking in.

I then suggested that it would be really important to write a lot and often *(setting up my next move, I hoped, with more intelligence gathering).*

While we were talking, a car pulled up.

It was Jose Osano from Chancellor Street 13; he was an ally of Oso's, and he went by "Chukas."

Oso went to his car, and I heard him whisper that he should leave because I was there, which he did.

I asked him why he told "Chukas" to leave, and he was startled that I knew who he was.

I told him that I'd been knee-deep in his ass for months; I knew everything about him—including the fact that he'd trusted the wrong people.

I said, "Coming to a new city, it was hard to know who you could trust and who you couldn't."

He yelled, "I knew it! Those fuckin' 18th Street bitches ratted us out! Fuckin' putos!" *(More head games and distrust successfully planted into his mind.)*

As we were talking, another vehicle drove past, this time a truck.

As it slowed down, Oso looked up.

I looked as well and recognized them as rival gang members: Juan Laredo and Roberto Quintana.

They were related but belonged to different gangs. Juan was St. Pauls 13, and Quintana was West Side Piru.

They started to yell at Oso, and he yelled back.

After they passed by, he said to me, "What are you gonna do about that? They just come by here and harass my family and me—and you fuckin' cops do nothing."

I thought this was funny: big badass gang member/leader wanted my help.

I didn't move, but I hung out the window of my car to watch them pass.

They stopped, and the passenger, Roberto Quintana, hung out the passenger window, looked right at me, then aimed a gun back towards us.

I thought he was aiming at Oso—but he was actually aiming at Oso's 2-year-old daughter.

Quintana shot and hit the girl as she stood on the side of the road a couple feet from me, and she dropped and started to scream.

I was really surprised by this, and for a brief moment I sat in disbelief; then, I felt this incredible feeling of rage surge through me.

I had to make a decision—and quick.

The truck was speeding away, and the girl was hurt, so I chose to chase the truck.

I was getting incredibly angry.

The edges of my vision were blackening, and tunnel vision started to creep in.

I remembered that a fire station was close to Oso's house, just around the corner, and that they had paramedics. I called out to dispatch and told them what had happened and to send medical to the house.

At the same time, I'd backed up my car and flipped around in a maneuver called a "J turn" to chase the truck.

I called out the direction of travel of the truck and tried to keep up with it in the hopes that another unit would intercept them; this, however, wasn't going to happen for some time.

Time slowed way down for me.

The chase seemed to go on for hours, but in fact it had only been maybe five minutes at the most.

I chased the truck though the city, running stop signs and crossing intersections at speeds hovering near 95 miles an hour.

I was raging, crazy pissed off; it was inexcusable to shoot a child in this gang warfare.

It made me even angrier that I knew both occupants of the truck and that they knew me and that I was present at the house—and in spite of that knowledge, they shot anyway.

I was furious.

I took this personally, wanting to fight and kill them both.

The law, the job, my family—it all went out the fucking window.

All I could think about was killing them both, but I'd have to catch them first—and I wasn't going to let them to survive this night.

They'd crossed the line and challenged me directly, doubting my response and my ability to rise to their level.

If I caught them, I was going to kill them...I was really fucking mad.

I was driving a small Chevy Cavalier, 4 cylinders, unmarked.

They had a GMC Sonoma pick up; needless to say, they left me behind with no problem.

When we reached an intersection at Reynolds and Jackson, they slowed way down, and I saw that they both turned to look at me as I approached.

I rolled down my window and yelled at them to stop and get out and fight; they looked at me, then looked at each other—and took off down Jackson.

I was out of my mind with rage.

I couldn't keep up in my car, and I called for any unit to help me catch them, but no one answered my call.

I was driving down Jackson Ave., running stop signs, gaining speed, and beating the hell out of my car.

Every intersection we crossed, the car slammed into the pavement, sending up sparks.

I could hear metal parts flying off the car and hitting the pavement, and I looked in the rearview mirror and saw metal parts flying up behind me; I hoped the car would hold together long enough to get me through the chase.

They never slowed down again, and I had a hard time keeping them in sight.

I called out again for another unit to help, but no one answered.

The truck reached the intersection of 43rd and Monroe, then went north.

Another police car was there, and it started to chase them as well—but the other cop was going too slowly, so I got on the radio and yelled at him to either get the fuck in the chase or get the hell out of my way.

He didn't respond, but he did speed up and gained on the truck, which then turned the corner at 43rd and Specker and pulled over.

I was out of my car immediately and approaching the shooter; in my mind, I saw images of me blowing his head off, then shooting the driver.

I walked up to the car and yelled at Quintana, saying, "Give me a reason to let you live, bitch."

He said nothing; he just looked at me and stared.

I wanted him to do something, say something, move—anything I could use for an excuse to shoot him.

But, he did nothing...he had no idea how bad I wanted to kill him right there.

I looked over at the other officer that had pulled the car over.

He was new; I didn't know him, so I had no idea what he'd say if I assassinated these two pieces of shit sitting in the car.

I was frustrated and angry.

I wanted the car stopped, but I also wanted to kill Quintana and Laredo.

I'd have to be satisfied with an arrest; that wasn't enough for me, but I had no choice.

I pulled Quintana from the car, still goading him, asking him to give me a reason to let him live; he said nothing.

I slammed him against the car and cuffed him, then walked him back to my car, dragging him by his hair and calling him a "fucking punk ass bitch."

I slammed him against my car and opened the passenger door, then put him in the car and cross-faced him while I put on his seat belt.

He started to complain, saying he'd have my badge for the cross-face move.

The stupid fucker had no idea I was way beyond that now; he was lucky to be breathing at all.

I grabbed him by the throat and told him I wanted to kill him right there, sitting in my car.

He was gagging and gasping for air; I had a tight hold on his throat, and he started to squirm and kick with his feet because he couldn't breathe.

His eyes were now wide with terror.

Inches from his face, I whispered, "What now, bitch? You gonna have my badge when you're fuckin' dead?"

I wanted to watch him die, and then I heard other cop cars approaching.

When I heard another cop say, "Hey, what's he doin' to that guy?" I knew I couldn't kill him.

I let go of his throat and slammed the door to the car with Quintana coughing and gasping for air inside.

I then called dispatch on the radio and checked the status of the little girl.

They said that she'd arrived at the hospital and was OK.

I was still out of control, though, so I just walked away from the scene.

I went about half a block, then grabbed a fence that was on the side of a construction site, holding on 'til I could think clearly again; screaming, cursing, and crying, I had nowhere to vent my rage.

Finally, I calmed down and went to the hospital.

I met with Oso there and told him that I'd caught the guys who shot his daughter and that I needed his help to convict them.

He was as angry as I was, pacing back and forth and screaming to the sky that he'd kill all the SP-13s.

I told him to stop, and after he saw how I was acting—how really truly angry I was—he stopped and listened.

I told him that I needed him to let me handle this, that there would be no payback until I got them into court and convicted; he could have his battle after the court dates were over, but not now.

He made no promises, but he said he'd think about it.

Meanwhile, his daughter would live.

She had injuries, but they weren't serious.

The bullet had punched through one arm, grazed her chest, and lodged in the other arm. She'd been really lucky; Quintana had aimed for a chest shot...he wanted her dead.

Oso called me on my cell phone a few days later and asked me to come to his house.

I met him out front; just as we'd been on the night of the shooting, my gun was again pointed at him.

He looked in and—seeing the gun—smiled.

"Sup, Ese?" he said.

I said, "Not much."

He said that he'd called a meeting with his set, CVL13, and Westside 18th Street. They talked over their options and decided that they wanted to go to war with the St. Pauls 13 gang for the shooting.

He said that he talked to them and convinced them to wait and see if I could get the guys who shot his daughter convicted; if I could, they'd take care of it in prison.

They weren't happy with him working with me, but they agreed to wait and see.

He asked me what I thought about that, and I told him I was cool with it.

"Just keep your ass off the streets so I can focus on getting them convicted," I said. "If I have one case cross my desk with your name on it, I'm coming after you—and the shooters will walk."

He glared at me long and hard, then finally said, "OK, Ese—you make that shit happen! You put those putos in the penitentiary; I'll do the rest."

Funny how quick we were able to become allies.

I still hated this guy, and he hated me—but we had an alliance now, a common goal...weird shit, how the street worked.

I was able to help convict both Quintana and Laredo of the shooting, and Oso kept his word and didn't start a gang war. I never had another case with him as a suspect again.

In the trial, I found out that Juan Laredo had a plane ticket out of the country to visit family in Mexico; he would have left early the next morning after the shooting.

He'd planned on doing the shooting, then leaving the country 'til things cooled off.

Roberto Quintana admitted that he'd shot at Oso's daughter on purpose, claiming that someone had shot at his kids and that he'd heard on the street that it was Oso.

He'd searched for him for some time and had finally found out that his cousin Juan knew where Oso lived.

They got drunk and went out that night, looking for Oso's house.

GREEN LIGHT ON PACMAN

WHILE I WAS WAITING FOR trial on this case, I had an informant call me and tell me that West Side 18th Street was having a meeting at Speedy's house.

They'd agreed to hold off on retaliation for Oso's daughter being shot; they felt that since he wasn't directly one of their gang members and was only an associate of theirs, they lost no face in letting the shooting go.

They did, however, feel that Smoker's arrest required a response, and my informant went on to tell me that they felt that I had to be taught a lesson for arresting him.

They hadn't had a member of their set arrested by the PD in some time.

They felt they had an arrangement with other gang cops, and they believed that they were immune from us; however, my arrest of Smoker had made a statement to them that this would no longer be the case.

The gang's leadership felt that they had to take action to protect the gang from me and make a statement of their own.

According to my informant, they'd agreed to meet at Speedy's house and make plans to kill me.

They were planning alibis, getting the logistics down as to who would do what and where...in short, they were planning a hit—on me.

As I pulled over and listened to this information, my informant was scared and out of breath.

We'd worked together on a lot of cases, and he was seriously afraid.

He said they were serious about it and that "they weren't fuckin' playing."

They'd even shaved their heads and dressed down. *(A statement meaning they were going to war.)*

They were serious and planned on doing the hit that day.

I still wasn't over the rage from the little girl being shot, and I have to admit I wasn't in my right mind.

This threat didn't make me afraid at all; instead, it only made me even angrier *(if that was possible).*

I sat on the side of the road and tried to think of what to do.

If I told the police department, they wouldn't believe me.

No one believed the gangs were this organized and disciplined; the cops foolishly believed that they were immune from gang violence.

I had nowhere to go with the information that was legitimate.

I drove past Speedy's house, and the yard was full of West Side 18th Street gang members' cars.

I started getting really pissed off.

I couldn't depend on the cops to help; they were so stupid about the street, I could never count on them.

So, I decided to deal with it myself.

I was getting more and more angry, less reasonable, and less coherent.

I called my informant and told him that I was going to take care of it myself.

I also told him to tell someone else about what he'd heard if I was killed.

He asked what I was going to do, and I told him that I didn't know yet.

I drove around for about five more minutes, mulling over different ideas.

Finally, I decided, *Fuck this!*

I went to Speedy's house and walked in on the meeting—with my gun out.

Speedy tried to kick me out of the house, but I pushed past him and told them all that I heard they wanted me dead.

There were at least twenty gang members there, and a lot of them I didn't know and had never seen.

They all had shaved heads and were dressed down, and they were quiet; no one said a word.

I said, "Word is, you fuckin' putos want me dead. Well, bitches, here I am—who the fuck do I kill first?"

After I got no response from the group, I said, "You fuckin' want me? Here the fuck I am! You aren't gonna sneak up on my ass on the street, shoot me in the back of the head, and drive off. We do this right *now*, motherfuckers!"

Still nothing.

The house was silent; no one moved, and no one said a word.

I said quietly, "Who the fuck is gonna step up and face me one-on-one?"

No one moved; they just stared at each other, then started talking to each other in Spanish.

One guy said I was fucking crazy and that he wanted no part of this.

Another one said that they should all rush me at once.

When I heard that, I said in English, "I agree, you should fuckin' rush me—who's gonna die first?"

I then yelled, "Come on, motherfuckers—let's *do* this!"

I started waving my gun, aiming it from one gang member's head to another, finger pulling on the trigger.

I wasn't bluffing; I'd really lost it. No one moved.

Finally, after about five minutes of this, I said, "If it even *looks* like one of you punk ass bitches is close to me—I'll kill your fuckin' asses. There will be no warning...I'll blow your fuckin' punk ass heads off. You bitches come near me—and you're fuckin' dead. Plan *that* into your fucking plans!"

I backed out of the house and left, then called my informant and asked him to keep his ears open.

After I told him what I'd done, I asked him to let me know what they decided to do.

He said, "Jesus, ESE! Are you fuckin' *crazy*?"

Ya, I guess I was crazy.

The girl being shot had changed me; I was really angry all the time.

A couple hours went by, and my informant called me back.

Laughing hysterically, he said they changed their minds!

He said that they decided I was fucking loco, and if they didn't succeed in killing me the first time that I'd hunt them all down and kill them all one at a time.

They said that because I was a cop—and crazy as well—I could get away with anything, so they called off the hit.

He said I scared the shit out of them, that they could see in my eyes that I was crazy and meant it that I wanted to fight right there in Speedy's house.

He was laughing so hard, he could barely talk.

He said, "Pacman, you really scared the shit out of them...you *are* fuckin' loco, ESE!"

I guess he was right...I *had* changed.

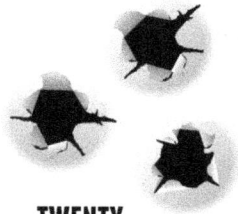

TODAY A SUSPECT, TOMORROW A VICTIM

SOMEWHERE IN-BETWEEN THE CVL13 CASE, these cases happened as well.

I got a call of a shooting at the 7-11 that used to be on the corner of 31st and Washington.

The victim was Juan Laredo *(this was before the drive-by on Oso's house).*

He was out with some girls and was pulling into the parking lot at a 7-11, which was popular to turn around in on the boulevard.

He was showing off his new car to the teenage girls there and didn't notice that there were several South Side 18th Street gang members in the parking lot.

He'd made several runs up and down the boulevard, showing off the car and getting noticed.

He then pulled into the parking lot to get some gas, going into the store to pay for it and get some food.

When he came out, "Evil" from South Side 18th Street was talking to the girls.

This really pissed Juan off, and he tried to pick a fight with "Evil", calling the South Side 18th Street gang member a sewer rat.

"Evil" got pissed off and shot at Juan, narrowly missing him.

Juan quickly left the parking lot in his car, and the store clerk called the police.

By the time I arrived, everyone was gone.

I took down the information from the clerk; he'd written down the license plate numbers of the vehicles involved and had told several witnesses to stay nearby 'til we arrived.

I took the statements from the witnesses and the clerk, then started to look for the suspect.

Initially, the scene had been very chaotic, and very few people actually knew who the shooter was or what he looked like.

Two girls said that they knew who the shooter was and identified him as "Angel"; he was a known South Side 18th Street associate.

I put together a photo lineup, and they both identified him as the suspect.

I went to his house, picked him up, and brought him to the station.

After several hours of interrogation, I determined that Angel wasn't the shooter; he'd been there, witnessed the shooting, and provided me with details of what had happened, but he wasn't the shooter himself.

He identified the shooter as "Evil" from South Side 18th Street, saying that until the shooting occurred, Juan was the aggressor in the incident and "Evil" had pulled out the pistol to protect himself from Juan because he was bigger than "Evil."

He did confirm, though, that Juan had no weapons.

The next night, I went to pick up "Evil" at his home.

Det. James *(the gang members called him "Powder")*, who was new in the unit at the time, accompanied me.

We went to the home and found no one there.

We got ready to leave the area, but I decided to wait *(that weird ass feeling again)*.

We sat by our cars for about five minutes, then "Evil" came around the corner in his parents' car; he was a passenger with his father and other family members in the car.

We stopped the car and removed Evil at gunpoint, taking him to the station.

I spent several hours with "Evil" but couldn't get him to confess; however, Powder took a crack at it and was able to get him to confess to the shooting in just a few minutes.

Evil was eventually convicted for the shooting.

During the trial, it was difficult to prosecute him because we now had cases pending with Laredo as a suspect as well.

This is one of the common problems with gang cases, and why it's so difficult to get successful prosecution: in one case, your victim is a cooperative—then a week later that same victim is now your suspect, and you're arresting them.

They're difficult and dynamic cases, and the gang world is constantly changing...your victim today is your suspect tomorrow.

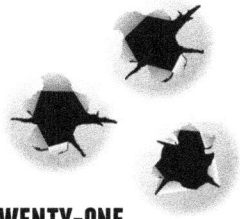

GANG CULTURE

THE ASIAN BROTHERHOOD HUNG OUT primarily in a neighboring county. They liked to frequent a Buddhist temple in the region, and they also had connections with Asian gangs in St. Erie and networked into California.

They were led by the Choi Family, which lived at 3600 Jackson Ave.

I had a couple informants in the gang and learned that they had an entirely different philosophy than the Hispanic gangs. For one, their initiation rite was totally different.

The Hispanic gangs had a process where prospective gang members were beat in; they had to face a group of fellow gang members that attacked them and beat them up.

Outnumbered, they had to show their "heart" and "toughness" by fighting the group until the allotted time had elapsed.

If they performed well, they were accepted.

The process was called being "jumped in."

The same brutal process was used to get out of the gang *("jumped out")*, only the beating was much more brutal.

For the Asian gangs, the process for prospective gang members to enter the gang was quite different: they were required to commit a crime.

The gang would choose a crime, usually either burglary, robbery, or rape, and the wannabe gang member would have to execute the crime as the gang described.

To me, this seemed to be a more intellectual approach to the gang banging life; show your ability to conduct crimes that would benefit the gang, such as enriching their monetary holdings or creating terror in a business owner to be "taxed" at a future time.

This difference spoke volumes to me about the Asian Brotherhood and their connections to other Asian gangs.

They had a culture and a "value system" consistent with Asian gangs all along the West coast.

They hadn't just randomly adopted a set of behaviors that seemed appropriate; they followed a well-established code of conduct.

St. Pauls 13, on the other hand, seemed to be a disorganized, chaotic mess.

Family cells were unaware of each other and frequently in direct conflict with each other; they each believed that "they" were the true St. Pauls 13 members and that the rest were just wannabes.

Each faction believed that they were tougher, smarter, and more "down" than the others in the set.

On the one hand this made them incredibly disorganized, but on the other it made them really hard to attack. They had no central leadership and no direction, and that made them difficult both to understand and defeat.

They also had no heritage.

They didn't know how the gang started or what the "13" meant in the name they yelled out so proudly.

They had no idea that it identified them as Sureneos *("Southerners")* when they entered the California prison system.

The California influence on St. Paul's gang culture is significant, and they seemed totally ignorant of this.

They professed to hate the Sureneos and referred to them as "sewer rats"; yet they carried the Sureneos identifier: "13."

They were a mystery to me.

Culturally, they were "poor" compared to the Asian gangs, unaware of their own gang's history.

On the other hand, 18th Street had some historical awareness of where the gang had originated and what the Sur 13 moniker meant.

Any 18th Street gang member I asked knew what the Sur 13 symbols meant, and they were just as baffled as I was by St. Pauls 13 gang members' ignorance of what the 13 in the gang's name meant.

I had several of them comment to me that "they call us sewer rats, but they're Sureneos just like us—what the fuck is wrong with them?"

South Side 18th Street was led by a distinct hierarchy.

The Gardenas family was the leadership of the set.

They were from California and were well known in the Hispanic community. The oldest, Brother Andy, was the leader of the set.

He was in and out of prison for drug distribution.

South Side 18th Street primarily focused on "making money."

They attempted to impose a street tax on residents in Central City, they were well known for drug distribution, and they had numerous connections to small, family-owned businesses that were rumored to be fronts for money laundering and drug selling.

West Side 18th Street was headed up by Jose Valencia, aka "Silent." They were a much smaller and more violent set than South Side.

South Side and West Side 18th Street had an uneasy alliance with each other; neither trusted the other, and both wanted to be in charge of the city.

GALLEGOS SPRAY AND PRAY

THE GALLEGOS HAD BEEN ONE of the dominant families in the St. Pauls 13 gang during the early nineties, and they'd suffered the consequences of being so heavily involved in the gang life.

The main Gallegos family faction of St. Pauls 13 had been led by Juan and Felipe Gallegos, who lived in a small, rundown house on the west side of the city.

They'd pretty much dominated the gang activities during the early 90s and had been victims of numerous drive-bys and gang fights.

First they fought with the SPVG gang, then with the Asian brotherhood, and finally with the 18th Street gang for dominance in the gang culture of the city.

After experiencing several negative incidents, the Gallegos finally withdrew from being the leaders in gang activity in the city.

First, Juan Gallegos attempted suicide then claimed to have been attacked by rival gangs when he survived.

He was in extreme depression from the toll the gang lifestyle had taken on his life, as well as the lives of his family and children.

Then, when it was discovered that he'd attempted suicide, he was thought of as weak and no longer a viable leader.

Also, the neighborhood gang members that the family had intimidated and threatened for years through their dominance of the gang became fed up with them, and they executed a very extensive drive-by on the Gallegos' home one day while the family was having a party in the front yard of their house.

There were numerous rounds fired, and well over forty casings were left in the street outside their house; using semi-automatic assault rifles and hand guns, the disgruntled gang members made a statement that they were no longer going to follow the Gallegos' lead.

I was assigned this case, and the family expected me to be able to solve it with no cooperation from them.

They'd developed a great working relationship with Det.'s Session and Rinker and expected that I'd follow suit and do whatever it took to make them happy, which was similar to the problem I had with 18th Street and the relationship that they had with Det. Jim Smally.

The Gallegos family expected preferential treatment from the police department, and they refused to cooperate with the investigation—yet still insisted that I "do something."

I was never able to get an arrest on the drive-by of their house, though, in spite of the fact that the entire family had been put at risk.

Surprisingly, no one was injured in the shooting; St. Pauls 13 was nowhere near as skilled at drive-bys as the CVL13 gang.

If CVL13 had done the shooting, I would have had several dead people in the front yard of the house.

ASIANS VS. TRECES

ANOTHER CASE I HAD WAS a gang fight between the Asian Brotherhood and members of the St. Pauls 13 gang that were aligned with the Gallegos.

The Gallegos were driving around the city one night and ran into the Asian Brotherhood.

The Gallegos had bought a yellow mid-80s Monte Carlo and had been showing it off in the city; the entire family was proud of the car and had been bragging about it to everyone they knew.

This particular night, the brothers Juan and Felipe had been out with cousin Jose Gallegos, aka "Batman."

While they were cruising the boulevard, they ran into the Asian brotherhood and began exchanging words and making comments about each other's cars.

The Asians would buy Honda or Nissan vehicles and work on the motors and body to make them into street rods. They didn't like Chevys, the Gallegos' favorite model of car.

The two groups ended up in the middle of the street, fighting in the middle of the night.

Jose Gallegos was stabbed several times and rushed to the hospital.

At the same time, an Asian kid named Diovanni Lee showed up with multiple stab wounds.

Neither group would cooperate with the investigation.

Both kids were injured with multiple stab wounds, but neither was seriously injured, and they went home after a few hours of observation.

Prior to this incident, Lee hadn't been identified as a gang member.

I went to his home and spoke to his parents, who had adopted him and his brother, David.

They confirmed that the boys had belonged to the Asian brotherhood, and they were at a loss as to what they should do; the boys had quit listening to them after joining the gang, and they felt that they had no influence over them.

No arrests were ever made in this case.

Without doing anything to help, the Gallegos again expected me to make arrests and get convictions.

They refused to allow me even to question Jose Gallegos, and statements were out of the question.

The Asians also never cooperated with the police.

They retained an attorney immediately for any case I had that involved them, or they simply refused to talk to me.

BLACK GANGS

WHILE WORKING THE HISPANIC GANGS, like St. Pauls 13, CVL13, South and West Side 18th Street, and the Asian gangs, as well as smaller gangs like 7th Street Mafiosos and SPCC *(St. Pauls' Craziest Chicanos)*, I also had to work the black gangs in the city.

We had a couple local gangs: "Doggden", a mixture of Bloods and Crips that claimed they controlled the Fred Marshal Center, and a loosely tied group of black dudes who were criminals, dealing drugs and making money but with no name to identify themselves.

Then there were the California gangs represented by members who had moved to the area either through Job Corps or "business opportunities" *(drug dealing)*.

My first contact with a transplanted California gang member was a mall security guard at the St. Pauls City Mall.

His name was Ray Riggins, and he was introduced to me through another police officer who worked part-time at the mall.

I used to hang out in the vicinity of the mall on my work days since it bordered my area and a lot of gang members would hang out there.

We used to talk, and I started to notice little things that he said and did that implied that he had an in-depth knowledge of the black gang members in the area, as well as the black drug dealers.

I started spending more and more time talking with him and learning from him, and eventually he opened up and admitted to me that he'd been a gang member in California and had moved here with Job Corps, which he'd entered to try to get away from California and make a better life for himself.

He said that he claimed East Coast 190 Crip and told me that he was one of many California gang members in the area.

Technically, he was still a gang member, but he'd curtailed some of his activities since he'd moved.

As our friendship developed, he showed me home movies of his brothers and other gang members at gang barbeques and parties.

During the videos, the family members were constantly throwing up gang signs and making cryptic gang comments.

He refused to wear anything red in color—ever.

I was surprised at how ingrained this aversion to the color red was in his mentality; even outside of California and in an environment that was relatively free of black gang-on-gang violence, he refused to wear red.

He began to open up to me about what was going on in the black community.

I'd been unable to develop any informants in the black community, and I had suspicions that there were numerous gang members in the city who hadn't been identified.

Over a period of several months, he confirmed that there were several different California sets represented in the city.

He told me about a correctional officer who worked in the jail. The officer was also an East Coast 190 Crip that went by the AKA "Lil Capone"; his real name was Paul Pogars.

He'd been working in the county jail for about two years and had taken the job for two reasons: he needed a job and had been hired by the sheriff's department, and he wanted access to the records kept in the jail about who was in jail, who visited the inmates, and how they could be contacted; this gave him inside information into the things that went on between the inmates, their attorneys, and the police.

I was quite shocked at how easy it had been for any gang member to infiltrate the corrections and police databases and facilities.

As I gained more and more of Riggins' trust, he began to loosen up and told me a lot of amazing things about how the police department and local correctional departments had been infiltrated by California gangs and local drug dealers.

As my awareness grew of what was going on behind the scenes, a lot more of what happened on the street made sense.

I understood why people who were really familiar with the street didn't trust cops and didn't believe we had any clue what was going on; we had no damn idea what was going on right under our noses.

Meanwhile, Paul Pogars worked in the jail and had access to all their records and databases.

Also, Riggins and two other guys worked in the mall and were closely associated with the police officers who worked there, and they talked daily to the cops who worked there part-time and gained their trust and confidence.

They knew everything that was going on at the police department and frequently rode around with the cops on duty when they *(the gang banger mall security guards)* weren't at work.

This gave them insight into how we worked and how much each guy really knew about the street.

The department had a very loosely monitored ride-along program, so they rode as often as they could to learn about the police.

STEVE TREMMEL

RIGGINS TOLD ME ABOUT A local guy whom he felt was running the worst scam of all.

He was bitter enemies with this guy; they both liked the same girl, "Kiki", and had been in fist fights and gunfights over her on several occasions.

The guy's name was Steve Tremmel, and he worked at Lost Creek, a juvenile lock-up for the more serious juvenile offenders in the area.

Tremmel bragged about how easy it had been to get into the system and use his position to locate and cultivate kids to distribute drugs in the community.

He was in a position in the facility to closely monitor the children and pick out the ones who he could most depend upon to keep his secret drug operation going; as a result, he cultivated a network that made him very rich.

I tried over and over again to get someone in Narcotics to listen to the information I had about Tremmel, but no one would listen.

I heard over and over again how impossible it was for the Juvenile corrections system to have been infiltrated so easily and that if that were true, their informants would have advised the Narcotics agents of it.

It was frustrating how stupid my peers were.

Riggins laughed when I told him about how Narcotics refused to look into Tremmel.

He said to me, "See! And you motherfuckers wonder why no one on the street trusts the cops?"

Finally, I mentioned Tremmel to Dirk Wiser.

He'd been recently assigned to the Narcotics section and had asked me if I knew of anything that had been missed by the previous group.

He spent a lot of time trying to get to Tremmel, and eventually he did; this was, however, years after the disclosure that Riggins had made to me.

T-BONE AND LOLLIPOP

RIGGINS ALSO TOLD ME ABOUT a California gang member who he said was the single biggest dealer of cocaine in the area.

His real name was James Bellweather. He used the alias "James McElroy" and had the gang name of "T-bone."

He was a Santana Block Crip from California and had formed an alliance with a local black drug dealer named "Sam."

I started to look into "T-bone" and began to monitor him closely.

I'd developed a pretty good understanding of who he hung out with and his pattern of behaviors.

I also checked with the Narcotics unit, and they'd heard of him.

Det. Mike Slacker had several cases pending on "T-bone" and had an informant who had made several buys of narcotics from him.

He hadn't been able to identify "T-bone" definitively, though, and without complete and correct identification he couldn't get an arrest warrant.

So, he asked me to keep an eye out for him.

T-bone liked to hang out at the American Legion at 38th and Aspen. It was a pretty much a "Blacks Only" bar with very few white people trusted and allowed inside.

He was very careful about who he sold to and did his business with a pager.

If you paged him, he called you back IF he recognized the number; if he didn't recognize the number, he wouldn't call you back.

He was very low profile and had made a name for himself on the street as a mellow, easygoing guy—as long as you didn't cross him.

He was also very likable and was trusted by a lot of people, which made him even harder to work my way into.

One night there was a shooting at the bar, and several cars were reported to have been leaving the area at a high rate of speed.

I was working the Central City at the time of the reported shooting and continued slowly towards the area.

I saw T-bone's white Chevy Monte Carlo approaching me at a high rate of speed; when he saw me, he slowed way down, dropping the nose of the car as he slammed on the brakes to drop speed.

As he turned the corner, I pulled him over.

This was the first time I actually had probable cause to stop him; he was leaving the scene of a shooting, traveling at a high rate of speed through a residential area.

I approached the car with my gun out and calmly told T-bone to keep his hands on the steering wheel.

I saw that he had his girlfriend in the front seat of the car and another drug dealer named Lollipop in the back seat.

"Lolli" was a little guy and was learning the "tricks of the trade" from "T-bone"; in effect, he was his apprentice—and he was armed, which I didn't find out 'til I was well into the stop.

Not that it mattered, though; by this time, I'd learned to treat every single person I ran into as if they were armed, no matter what the circumstances.

I asked T-bone to get out of the car and follow me to the rear of the vehicle.

He had no identification.

I knew that he never carried any; that was how he kept himself anonymous on the street.

No one ever knew his real name: "James Bellweather"; "T-bone" was how his closest friends knew him—and that's all they knew.

I played dumb with him, not letting him know what I already knew about him.

I told him that I needed to know who he was and that since he was driving, I needed a valid driver's license.

He admitted to me that he didn't have one.

I searched him for weapons and found none.

He did have a pager *(the pager he used to conduct his business)*, so I asked him the number to it and warned him that I'd call it to verify whether or not he'd been truthful.

He gave me the number to the pager, and I called it from the cell phone that I kept in my car. He'd given me the correct number; we were establishing trust.

I asked him if he'd been at the Legion bar, and he said that he had been, but "all kinds of drama had busted loose," so he left.

I told him that was the reason I'd stopped him; he was traveling away at a high rate of speed from a report of shots being fired at the Legion.

He replied that it made sense to him.

This all went into my report to justify the stop.

I asked him if there were any weapons in the car, and he said that no one had weapons in the car.

I told him that, due to the nature of the stop, I'd have to search the car.

He agreed and even gave me permission to search it.

I did find a Lorcin 380 in the back seat where Lolli had been sitting, and I approached "T-bone" and said, "What the fuck is this, man?"

He instantly transformed from calm "T-bone" to angry "T-bone" and confronted "Lolli," saying to him "I told you no guns, motherfucker!"

"Lolli" was a prick and said, "Fuck that shit, man! Quit kissing this cop's ass; he can't prove shit."

"T-bone" quietly turned to me and said, "I didn't know he had a gun, and I apologize for it."

I didn't know what to think of him.

There he was, mellow as hell to me and angry with his friend for having a gun.

I didn't expect that from him; I was ready to go to war with the guy, ramped up to battle with his drug-dealing ass.

I could see why he was so trusted by the people on the street; he may have been a drug dealer, but he was very real.

Criminal? Yes. Asshole? No.

Regardless, I told him that I'd have to book him into jail because I couldn't verify who he was.

I told him that if he had a driver's license I would have been able to release him on a citation, but that it was state law that if I couldn't identify him I had to book him into jail.

He said that he understood and asked that I release his car to his girlfriend.

It wasn't legal for me to do that, and if things had gone differently I have to admit I would have fucked him over any way that I could, impounding his car and digging for some way to make his life more miserable.

To me, attitude was everything. Treat me with respect, and I'll return it; treat me like shit, and I'm gonna find any way possible to make you hate the day I was born.

So I did release the car to T-bone's girl after I checked "Lollipop's" gun to see if it was stolen.

It wasn't, and it also wasn't loaded.

I had no reason to keep it or arrest him, so I let him leave with "T bone's" girlfriend and car.

I then transported T-bone to the jail, and we talked on the way.

I have to admit, I liked the guy; he was very likeable, and he was the biggest dealer in the city for a reason: he was very smart and articulate.

I booked "T bone" into jail and specifically asked that he be fingerprinted; that was unusual for a no driver's license charge, and I had to explain why to the intake officer.

I asked that the card be forwarded to Det. Slacker in the hopes that "T-bone's" real identity would be discovered.

They agreed and fingerprinted "T-bone", then released him on bail to his girl.

The information I'd been given by Riggins was correct, and I began to rely heavily on him for more.

I told him about my stop of "T-bone", and he said that "T-bone" had told him about the stop as well.

He said that they played video games together often and that "T-bone" told him about how he'd been doing business *(dealing drugs)* in the city for several years and that the cops had never caught on to him because he was careful and smart.

He said that "T-bone" made the comment that the cops in this area were really stupid compared to California and that it was easy to stay out of jail.

He laughed about the stop that I'd made, bragging that he'd gotten away again without being identified.

He laughed and said, "That cop booked me under my fake name! They'll never catch me!"

A few days later, Slacker got a hold of me and thanked me for the stop.

He'd positively identified "T-bone" as James Bellweather.

Having pulled his record and found that he'd done time for a murder in California, he was able to convict Bellweather for the drug deals that he'd done in the city and sent him to prison.

I ended up using "T-bone's" opinion of how stupid the cops in St. Pauls were to my advantage.

I hung out and started to push my contact with him, tailing him in my area and stopping to talk to him whenever I could.

I learned a lot about him and who he hung out with, as well as how he continued to sell drugs right up until he was sent to prison.

"T-bone" started to trust me and even asked that I write a letter to the parole board to help him get an early release; I did whatever it took to cultivate informants, so hell ya, I wrote the letter.

"T-bone" later confided in me that his attorney had tried to pick up on his girlfriend after he was incarcerated. He felt really betrayed by that; he hired the man because he was highly recommended.

"T-bone" found out the hard way what we cops already knew: attorneys were no one's friends. It took a very "special" kind of person to be an attorney.

Anyway, after that "T-bone" asked that I keep an eye on his girl while he was locked up and let him know if she was seeing someone else. I did look out for her, and when I saw her going frequently to "Sam's" place to buy cocaine, I let him know.

He sent her a letter telling her that I was watching and that she needed to quit going to the drug house; I knew all of this from the faxes I was getting from the prison.

He told her that he was gonna go straight and that they'd move from the area when he got out.

They kept in touch, and he was given an early release from prison.

I met him in the mall later, after he'd been released.

He walked up to me and shook my hand, thanking me for what I'd done for him.

I don't know what he thought I'd done to deserve that; I had been the one that had identified him and ultimately enabled him to be imprisoned—but like I said, we clicked.

RON RON HUBBARD

RIGGINS TOOK ME UNDER HIS wing and tried to explain the streets to me from his point of view.

One day, he told me about a guy he respected tremendously, Ron *(Ron Ron)* Hubbard.

He described Ron as another drug dealer in the area who was an L.A. gang member. He said that Ron claimed Palm and Oak Crips, and that he had quite a reputation on the street as a drug dealer and a fighter.

He told me about an incident between Ron and a local dealer named Perry Willer, which occurred at the American Legion.

Perry had been talking all kinds of shit on the street about Ron, saying that he was a "punk" and a "bitch" and that he *(Perry)* was gonna take over his drug trade.

Ron had gotten word of this and confronted Perry in the American Legion, choosing the bar for a reason; he wanted to make sure that no one doubted who he was and what he was capable of.

He confronted Perry and beat him up badly, making sure everyone in "his world" saw it. *(He didn't want anyone thinking he was a bitch.)*

After beating his ass down, Ron made Perry apologize to him and call him "Sir" in front of everyone at the bar.

Having made his point, he then walked away.

Riggins told me about this and laughed about Perry and how Ron had called him out on his shit talking.

He admired Ron for his toughness, and he said that when he wasn't beating your ass, Ron was really cool.

I started to look into "Ron Ron" and found that he lived on the west side with his father, who was a heroin addict. .

"Ron Ron" watched out for him and tried to keep him clean.

His father rented the house from a local church, and I started to keep an eye out and waited for a call or an incident to occur there so I could have a reason to get in and talk to Ron.

Several months went by, then one night I heard a call dispatched to patrol to report that a man had called the police to claim that he'd been beaten up.

The address was Ron Ron's, so I took the call, jumped in, and headed down to the house.

I cancelled the back that was sent so that I wouldn't have anyone screwing up this rare opportunity.

I met with the victim, who identified himself as Andrew McElroy.

He claimed that he'd been beaten up by Ron, then thrown out of the house.

He said that he'd lived in the house with Ron and his heroin addict father for several months and that Ron had kicked him out for disrespecting his father.

Andrew said that he knew his rights and that he was a victim of domestic violence; he'd been a co-habitant with Ron and had been physically beaten up by him, so he wanted Ron arrested for the DV assault.

I did see that Andrew had a minor cut on his lip, and it appeared that he might have been hit in the mouth.

So, I checked with Ron and heard his version of the story.

It was my first meeting with Ron, and I was sizing him up to see if he measured up to what Riggins had told me.

Ron was very straightforward about the incident, saying that he'd kicked Andrew out for calling his father an addict and for not paying rent.

He said that he asked him to leave several times, but that had Andrew refused; so, Ron said he picked him up and forced him out of the house.

He said that Andrew tried to hit him, and he blocked the punch and "popped him once in the mouth to get his attention"—and that was the end of the fight.

After that, Andrew ran off and started to cry.

Ron called him a "whining bitch", and I had to admit that he was a whining bitch; he was literally crying as well—and he was really getting on my nerves.

I talked to Ron a little longer and noticed that he had tattoos on the backs of his arms; there was a "P" and an "O" in dark black ink.

I asked him what the tattoos were, and he said that he was a Palm and Oak Crip from Los Angeles.

I suspected that he'd been telling me the truth from the beginning, and now he was admitting his gang membership freely.

I was starting to like this guy!

Honesty and an "I don't give a damn attitude" always made it easy for me like people.

I decided to check on Andrew and see if he had warrants.

After I found out that he did have one, I arrested him for it.

I added what he'd told me about the assault into the report but didn't arrest Ron for it.

I told Ron that I'd heard about the incident at the Legion Club and was well aware that if he wanted to beat Andrew's ass, he could have.

I also told him that I agreed that Andrew was a whining bitch and that I wasn't gonna arrest him *(Ron)* for the assault.

Ron was alarmed that I knew about the assault at the club and asked me what I'd heard.

I told him that I knew someone who had witnessed it, but I didn't tell him who had told me about it.

He asked that I come back after booking Andrew into jail and talk to him some more, and I did just that.

When I returned, we talked 'til morning *(several hours)*.

He freely admitted that he dealt drugs and that his father was a heroin addict.

He also told me that he and a few other gang members from California had been in the area dealing drugs for some time.

I told him that I was mainly interested in gangs and had no interest in his drug trade.

He told me all about "Doobie", "T bone", "Lollipop", and a guy named "Boo Rock", saying that they were all "businessmen"—meaning drug dealers.

He said that his real name was Ronald McElroy and that he'd used the name Ron Hubbard because it was easy to remember; the real Ron Hubbard was famous, and that would confuse the cops if they ever heard anyone talking about him.

It was a really interesting night; he was quite upfront about his business and what he did.

He said that it was getting tougher and tougher in the street for the black dealers to make money dealing drugs; the reason being, the Hispanics had moved in and taken over, which made it harder for the blacks to maintain dominance in the drug trade.

He specifically named 18th Street and EME *(The Mexican Mafia)* as being present in the city.

He said that he had drug charges pending and that he knew he was headed to prison and would probably never see his father again.

He said that he wanted me to know that the 18th Street gang was taking over the streets and that they'd been running restaurants and small stores.

He also knew that they had large sums of money buried in the yards of houses that they owned.

He went on and on about them, how they worked the drug trade and laundered money, bringing drugs into the country when they bought supplies for their stores and restaurants from Mexico.

He was amazingly open and upfront about his gang membership and drug dealing; he wasn't ashamed at all of what he did.

He said that he was "a gang banger and a thug and that dealing was only about money."

It was a business to him.

He had the old school value system of gangs and street behavior; they had a code that they lived by, a distinct value system.

This is now gone from the street, and the only value system is centered on the value of money and surviving the moment.

When I left that morning after talking to him for several hours in the front yard of his house, I was in a daze; it was always a trip to talk to someone that you should hate and really despise—but instead find yourself identifying with them and liking them more than your fellow cops.

I had more in common with Ron than I had with 95% of the cops I worked with.

The next time I saw Ron Ron, he was in court; he was there to get sentenced and saw me in the courthouse on another case.

He came over to me and shook my hand, then told me to take care.

He said that the next time he'd be free, we'd both be old men and that we'd go get a beer and talk about the streets when we were younger.

The reaction this caused in the people in the courtroom was comical because he did it right in front of a bunch of cops.

They all looked at me with their eyes wide open and jaws dropped.

"Ron Ron" didn't talk to anyone—much less a cop in uniform; however, he'd shaken my hand and openly talked with me as a friend.

This was another one of those priceless moments where it was painfully obvious that I didn't fit in on either side of the alleged thin blue line.

TWENTY-EIGHT

DOOBIE

DOOBIE WAS AN L.A. GANG member who came into the city in the early nineties.

He'd been dealing cocaine and eventually was caught and sent to federal prison.

He had quite a reputation on the street as a scrapper, and he came back to St. Pauls after serving his time and made a real attempt to stay straight.

I got a call to his house one night.

He'd been working a job as a semi-skilled laborer for a company in the industrial area in Widefield, and his boss had been really impressed with his work ethic.

Doobie showed up for work one night, and the boss told him to go home, saying that since they were way ahead of their projected output, he was giving him the night off.

He also said that Doobie had been the biggest reason for that output and that he'd be providing Doobie's parole officer with this feedback.

He was really impressed with the job that Doobie was doing, and he was one of the best—if not *the* best—workers that he had.

Doobie was really happy; finally, his life had started to turn around.

He'd bought in to the whole "work hard to get ahead, stay clean" philosophy, and it was working for him.

Maybe he could make this new life work for him (*his words*). He came home happy, "sincerely happy", for maybe the first time in his life.

He was living with and/or married to his girl, who had stayed with him through prison.

She had his children, a boy and a girl. They'd gotten back together when he got out of prison, and he was trying to be a father and a husband.

This was new territory for him, and for the first time in a long time, he liked how he felt.

He was excited to tell his girl about his latest success and spend an extra night with the kids; however, when he pulled up to his house and walked to the front door, he said he looked through the glass in the door and thought that he'd mistakenly gone to the wrong apartment.

Why? Because he saw his kids watching TV on the living room floor—and his wife in the same room with his two best friends.

She was giving one a blowjob while the other was fucking her from behind.

He said that he was stunned; he couldn't believe what he was seeing.

All this was happening in the same room as his children watching TV.

They were on the floor in front of it while their mom was being tag teamed by his two best friends.

He walked through the door and beat serious ass.

He beat the shit out of his two "friends"—I mean *really* beat them up bad—then he went to work on the wife, beating the hell out of her.

He was in a rage; he'd been in prison and had been a real gangbanger from L.A.—and he knew how to fight.

I got the call from a neighbor who heard the fighting.

When I arrived and tried to ask the wife what had happened, she wouldn't tell me anything.

Doobie just sat on the front porch and said nothing.

The wife had been beaten up, and finally he said to me, "I beat her ass."

I asked what had happened, and he wouldn't say.

I then arrested him, and he went with me quietly.

On the way to the station, he was in shock and really acting weird, so I pulled over in the vacant parking lot of a place that had recently gone out of business.

I started to talk to him, and he started to cry; at first it was just a little bit, then he sobbed and really broke down.

He told me what had happened, how he'd bought into the whole "work and live right and your life will turn around" ...he was totally devastated, an emotional wreck.

I let him sit in my car and cry for several hours.

He told me all about his life, selling drugs and prison life, and how he'd tried to turn it around, "do the right thing," and "come correct."

I listened, and after a while I knew I wouldn't arrest him; I'd probably get fired, but instead I wrote the assault up as a minor assault so that I could release him on a misdemeanor citation.

In my report, I minimized the beating and didn't fully explain his wife's injuries.

I told him that he was doing the right thing, that he was living the right way—but that he had to realize a few facts.

He had changed, but his wife had *not*.

I'd seen this often while I was in gangs: the guy (*gang member*) would change and expect that the wife or girlfriend would be OK with it—but they weren't.

The women who are attracted to gang members have a whole different set of issues of their own.

Most liked the element of danger when it comes to being around a gang member; the constant chaos and danger were addicting.

When that thrill was gone, they turned to sex, drugs, and betrayal of the gangster.

If Doobie wanted to go back, they had a lot of shit to work out.

I asked him if he wanted to go back, and he said that he did.

So, when he was ready, I took him back to the house, met with both of them, and told them what I was gonna do.

The wife then went to a friend's house, and Doobie stayed in the apartment.

I told him that I didn't know what his P.O. would do, but I wouldn't put him in jail because that would violate him for sure and he'd go back to prison.

I don't know what happened to him; I never saw him again.

I never regretted the decision I made not to arrest him, though, and I never went to court on the ticket, nor did I ever get a call from his P.O.

TWENTY-NINE
BOO ROCK

ANOTHER NIGHT AT THE LEGION, and another fight had broken out.

This time, I arrived at the Legion and found that there were several people still there, milling around.

Two guys had been seriously injured and were about to be transported from the scene to the hospital; one of them had received a severe stab wound on the side of his head and was bleeding profusely.

I spoke to the girl who was helping him and asked her what had happened.

She refused to talk to me, but she did follow him to the hospital.

I knew that her name was Sandy Stafford and that it was well known in the black community that she dated only black men and was one of the few whites trusted and allowed in the American Legion club.

I followed the ambulance as well and hung around the Emergency Room in plain clothes, minus my gun and badge, to see what I could learn.

Sitting in a chair and reading a magazine, I listened to what was going on.

I soon overheard three people talking to Sandy in the hallway.

She told them that "Bobby," "Ebony," "Bay," and Gary Wright had arrived at the club with several of their friends; they'd come to fight with several of the California Gang bangers who had recently moved into the area and were trying to expand on their drug trade.

She said that they'd told "Boo" that he wasn't in California any longer and that he needed to show respect to the "brothers" who were here.

She said that Boo had gotten into an argument with Bobby and that Bobby broke a bottle and stabbed him in the head.

I had all I needed to go talk to "Boo."

I took the back way through the Emergency Room and went into his room, where I introduced myself and told him that I was there to check the facts of what happened.

I asked him if he was OK.

He replied, "Yes, sir, I am."

California gang bangers are almost always incredibly polite.

This was my second clue that he was, in fact, from California.

I recounted what I'd heard in the hallway and used the name "Boo" when I referred to him.

He acknowledged that he'd been in a fight with Bobby Snyder.

He didn't react to me using his street name, "Boo"; this was so much a part of his identity that it was second nature, and he hadn't realized what had just happened.

He said that Snyder had jumped him at the Legion, and I asked if it was about "business and respect."

He said it was.

He said, "Damn, man, how do you know all this?"

I played like I'd been watching him for weeks and knew all about him.

I told him that I had informants in the Black community and knew that he went by the name "Boo rock."

I also told him that I was aware that he was a "businessman" and that this fight was about business.

He nodded his head in agreement to both facts; he didn't deny he was "Boo rock," and I continued to refer to him as "Boo" as he gave me the complete story of what had happened.

I asked him if he wanted to press charges, and he rolled his eyes at me and replied, "niggah please."

I said, "Hey, I have to ask."

He said, "Hell no, I will *not* press charges. I ain't no bitch. I'll deal with this in my own way."

I said, "OK. Anything else you wanna tell me?"

He said, "No."

I said, "If I need to get a hold of you, will you be staying at Sandy's place?"

He just stared at me and said, "Damn, man—you *have* been watchin' me! Ya, that's where I stay."

I knew that "Ebony" was the street name for Doug Croates and that he was a known associate of Bobby Snyder. "Bay" Stewart was Will Stuart, and Gary Wright was an 18-year-old kid who had been hanging around them lately.

I was able to get a copy of the name that Boo rock had given the Emergency Room and ran him for NCIC warrants.

He had a hit out in California; he was wanted for an Aggravated Robbery. I used that to gain Sandy's trust later when I went to her house.

I tried to follow up on the case but couldn't get anyone to cooperate.

I went to Sandy's house a few days later and talked to her and "Boo rock."

I told them that the case was dead but that I'd done some checking and that he was wanted in California on an Aggravated Robbery charge.

They tensed up, and I told them that I'd keep that on the down low for now; I was mainly interested in gang information and wanted to know what they could tell me.

They didn't tell me anything, claiming that they didn't know anything about the local gangs; that was a mistake. I'd been straight with him and had given them both breaks—but I would *not* be played like a punk. Work with me, and I could be a friend; cross me, and you're in deep shit.

I left, then called the Narcotics Strike Force and told them about "Boo Rock," telling them that I had an informant that gave me his real name.

I also said that I'd checked and that he had a warrant as well. I told them that I'd heard that he was a major dealer and lived with Sandy Stafford.

They'd been working him but didn't know his name, so with the information I gave them *(his name and the place he was staying)* they arrested him a few days later on a search and arrest warrant.

When I went to see Sandy a few days later, she was crying; Boo had been arrested, and she was alone again. She talked to me for quite a while, telling me her life story.

From that point on, she waved when I drove past, and if she was at a scene involving the Black community and I saw her, I'd later go to her house and she'd give me information on what had happened. She never knew that I was the one who gave up Boo Rock and that I got almost all my information on him from her.

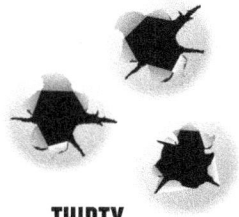

BANK ROBBERIES

ONE NIGHT, RIGGINS GOT A hold of me and wanted to meet somewhere away from the mall.

I was immediately on guard and started thinking that I needed to cover my ass; was he gonna try to get stupid with me?

I didn't know what he had planned, but I went prepared to kill him if necessary; I was sure he was setting me up.

That's the nature of a cop's relationship with informants; it's based on a twisted kind of trust that can dissolve in a heartbeat.

I arrived at a car wash in a nearby city where he wanted to meet.

He was alone and really agitated, and he said that he'd heard some shit that he wanted to get off his chest.

He told me that he'd been at a party at Snyder's house the previous week and had overheard some kid talking about doing bank robberies.

He'd thought the kid was full of shit and blew him off until he saw on the news that a bank robbery had, in fact, happened.

He didn't know the guy's name and didn't feel like he could ask around since he was "an out of town niggah" *(meaning, since he was a gangbanger from California, he had only limited trust in the local community).*

He felt sure that the kid had done the bank robbery, saying that he was "fucking crazy" and was "waving a gun around at the party," calling himself "Superman" and saying that he was "bulletproof."

The kid had really gotten him upset.

I listened to him, but I was suspicious.

I'd arrived there at the car wash expecting to get into a gunfight with him and whoever he was with; instead, I found him alone and wanting to talk about a bank robbery.

I asked him why the secrecy and he said that the kid had really shaken him up.

He said he was really worried that the kid was gonna kill someone and that he truly believed the kid thought he was invincible.

I asked another informant about the kid, whose street name was "Dazzle."

He said that he'd been at the party as well and was surprised that I'd heard about it.

He admitted that there was a kid there who was bragging about doing a series of bank robberies that had occurred in the past few weeks.

He said that the kid hung out with Bobby Snyder and had recently bought one of the new Toyota Land Cruisers, claiming that he paid cash for it.

He said for me to keep my eye out at the Center City 7-11, and I'd see him there; he liked to go in there and show off the car.

I asked if "Dazzle" had seen the Land Cruiser.

He said that he had and that it was nice.

I asked him if he knew what the kid's name was, and he said he only knew that he went by "Gary."

I started to hang out at the 7-11, waiting for Gary to show up.

A few days later, he did—and he did have a really nice Land Cruiser. I complimented him on the car and asked him if I could look inside.

He said, "Sure, go ahead. I'm goin' inside the store to get some grub."

It was immaculate, and while I admired it I wrote down the VIN so I could run it to see if it was stolen.

He came back out and told me, "You in the wrong line of work, PoPo."

I said, "No doubt, man, this is nice! How much did you pay for it?"

He said, "Fitty large," meaning 50 thousand.

I asked, "How the hell can you afford this, Gary?"

He didn't bat an eye that I'd called him Gary.

He said, "Gary Wright has his ways, Po Po...he has his ways."

He then smiled and left the parking lot.

I ran the VIN and license plates, making sure they belonged to each other.

I then checked the car to see if it was stolen.

It wasn't; in fact, it was registered to Gary.

I contacted the detectives in St. Pauls who were working with the FBI on the robberies.

They were working with the SPCAT (*St. Pauls Criminal Apprehension Team*) as well.

SPCAT was a multi-jurisdictional unit that worked with the FBI in tracking down only the most serious criminals.

I advised them of what I'd been told by Dazzle and Riggins—but I didn't disclose who had told me, only that "informants" had put me on to it.

They told me that I was out of my mind if I thought some fucking 18-year-old kid could have done these robberies; they'd been "professionally done" and couldn't have been the work of "some stupid fucking kid."

I wasn't surprised at their arrogance; I was getting used to how incredibly stupid my peers were, and this wasn't gonna be an exception.

I dropped it, and a few days later when I heard Gary was arrested by the FBI for the robberies, I wasn't surprised.

I later talked to Dazzle, and he said that Snyder had given the kid up to the FBI.

He also said that Snyder was "in their pockets" and "had been for some time."

A light went on in my head.

Snyder had done an ass load of crimes in the area; he'd been caught in sting after sting, selling stolen property, stolen cars, and drugs—but he never served more than a month or two before he'd be back out of jail.

He never went to prison for anything and now it made sense: Snyder was a snitch who would give up his friends to keep himself out of jail.

This was exactly what his father had done to stay out of jail as well.

Now that I thought about it, it was painfully obvious.

I don't know if it was true or not; I was never able to confirm it.

I was, though, able to confirm that Gary was arrested for the bank robberies.

THIS DJ AND DIRTY LEFT

ONE NIGHT, I WAS HANGING out at the mall talking with Riggins and Pogars.

When they mentioned going to a party with Snoop Dog's step-brother, "Dirty Left," I thought they were full of shit—and I told them just that.

They were both really offended and said that they weren't lying.

I said, "OK, you show me a picture of motherfuckin' 'Dirty Left' and you together, and I'll believe you."

Pogars said that he did have pictures of him and "Dirty Left," but even more than that, he'd been invited by "Dirty Left" to go to Snoop Dog's house in about a month and hang out.

I said to them, "OK. You show me pictures of you at Snoop's, and I'll believe it."

Pogars had never talked to me about anything.

I waited for him to leave, then asked Riggins about the claim to know Left.

He said that Pogars was really the one who was friends with "Dirty Left" and that when Pogars had told him that he was hanging with Snoop's brother, he hadn't believed him either.

Pogars introduced Riggins to "Dirty Left" at the Legion one night.

Initially, Riggins didn't believe that this guy was Snoop Dog's brother, but then he started to listen to the guy's story.

According to Dirty Left, he was Snoop Dog's half-brother.

They'd grown up together, and when Snoop became famous he'd asked Dirty Left to move away; the whole East Coast vs. West Coast rap thing was getting really heated in California, and Snoop thought rival gang bangers might try to kill or kidnap Dirty Left to get to him.

So, "Dirty Left" moved to Pine Valley, a city near St. Pauls.

He was arrested for an Aggravated Robbery there and did some time.

After he was released, he stayed in the state and occasionally went back to California to visit Snoop.

Riggins said that Dirty Left had shown them pictures of him and Snoop together in Snoop's house, standing on the "Dog Pound" logo in the carpet.

Riggins said that he then believed Dirty Left's claims.

I heard these stories about Dirty Left for a few weeks, then one day Pogars showed me his own pictures.

They included him, Snoop Dog, and another guy in swim suits hanging out at a pool.

He said the third guy was Dirty Left.

He then showed me a picture of all three of them and the "Dog Pound" logo in Snoop's carpeting.

I was amazed; again, I'd found more information linking the gangs in St. Pauls to the gangs in California—and now big names in California—and had no one to tell who would believe me.

As far as casework was concerned, this had no law enforcement value, but it did show a significant connection to major gangs on the West Coast.

A few weeks later, Riggins gave me a calendar.

In it were pictures of two Long Beach gangs.

One was a set that included Dirty Left, Snoop Dog, Nate Dog and Warren G; the other was another gang that they were rivals with.

The two gangs had called a truce, agreeing not to kill each other, and they made a calendar to try to spread the peace of the truce to other gangs in the area.

The different months of the calendar showed pictures of gang members in each set whose lives had been affected by the gang life.

There was only one picture of Snoop and Dirty Left.

They were identified in the picture by gang name—and they were the same two faces I saw in Pogars' pictures of him with Snoop by the pool, as well as in Snoop's house.

I asked Riggins if he could get me "Dirty Left's" real name, and he said that he'd try.

A few weeks later, he came to me and told me "Dirty Left's" real name, and I looked it up and did a "III" check; as a result, I found out that there was an aggravated robbery charge in Pine Valley City assigned to that name.

I then looked up the name "Dirty Left" on the Web and found that there was a song by Warren G that referenced "Dirty Left"; it was called "This DJ."

This was the kind of amazing shit that went on right under the police department's nose, but no one would believe it or have any idea of what it meant for the gang culture in the city.

By way of Pogars and Riggins, legit hardcore California gang members were hooked up to our databases and knew the way we operated.

THIRTY-TWO

DOGGDEN VS. SOUTH SIDE 18TH STREET

I HAD VERY LITTLE CONTACT with Doggden.

I theorized that they were a collection of local Black criminals who dealt drugs, sold stolen property, partied at the American Legion, and hung out at Bobby Snyder's house—but I was never able to prove that; I just didn't have the time to devote to gathering that kind of intelligence on them.

The only significant activity I had with them involved South Side 18th Street and the Fred Marshal Center.

The Fred Marshal Center was a youth center named after a cop who had been killed during a hostage situation.

Having grown up in the city, he was a "home grown cop" and was thought of very highly in the community.

To the best of my knowledge, the center was never clearly claimed by any gang.

It had very strong ties to the Black community, and the police department felt like they were welcome there as well; reality was, the cops were just tolerated.

The people who ran the center were very leery of them, and after I became more aware of how deeply we'd been infiltrated by criminal elements, as well as how many dirty cops there were, I understood this fear.

We were completely stupid and unaware of what was really going on in the streets.

Some time during the summer of that year, South Side 18th Street made a push to take over the Fred Marshal Center.

They started by showing up in groups and hanging around, which made the people who frequented the center uneasy.

Then 18th Street started being more aggressive, throwing up gang signs and writing South Side 18th Street gang graffiti on the benches and basketball courts outside the building.

Finally, they started to harass women and children in the area.

I was made aware of all this when shootings started to occur.

It turned out that two to three South Side 18th Street gang members had walked up to several Doggden members and told them the center was theirs; the Doggden crew, though, had no intention of letting the 18th Street gang take it over.

18th Street gang members then started doing their usual show of gang signs and shit talking to the "Doggden" members, but the Doggden members weren't impressed or afraid of the 18th Street gang members, instead pulling out guns and starting to shoot.

No one was hit, but the point was made.

A few days later, the 18th Street gang retaliated and shot at several Black guys and their families who were hanging out in the park; again, no one was hit.

The 18th Street gang yelled out their gang's name during the shooting to let the whole area know that they meant to take over the center and that their gang was responsible for the shooting.

Doggden retaliated immediately—and much more dangerously.

They weren't fucking around; they made it really clear that if 18th street wanted a war, it would be an all-out, no holds barred event.

They targeted an apartment complex near the center where several 18th Street gang members lived; instead of targeting the gang members themselves, though, they went after the women and children—including infants.

This was getting out of hand.

Within a day, I received word through an informant that the mother of the Gardenas family wanted to talk to me about the incidents.

So, I went to her home and spoke to her.

I was expecting her to ask me what I planned to do about the shootings and why hadn't I arrested the Doggden gang members; instead, she asked me in a very roundabout way if there was anything I could do about the shootings.

I wasn't on good terms with the Gardenas family.

They were very full of themselves as a group and didn't like me as a detective in the gang unit.

It took some time for her to get to the point that she was trying to make. In a nutshell, she asked that I contact the members of Doggden, preferably their leadership, and negotiate a truce; I couldn't believe what I was hearing. *(This was a true "WTF" moment.)*

I told her that I had no idea who the leaders of the group were.

I then said, "From what I understand, your guys set this bullshit up and tried to take over the Fred Marshal Center. Why the fuck should I help you out now?"

She said that one of the infants that was nearly killed in the previously mentioned attack was a friend's child and that she didn't want any children injured.

She again asked that I talk to the Doggden gang members and call off the fight.

She claimed to be able to guarantee that South Side 18th Street would withdraw from the center and that no more graffiti or shootings would occur from their set.

I told her that if I and my name were gonna be involved, she'd better be able to do what she claimed.

She again said that she could guarantee that the activities would cease.

We looked at each other long and hard.

Neither of us said a word; there was lots of nonverbal communication going on, but nothing being said.

We hadn't had the kind of relationship that would warrant this kind of trust; we didn't like each other at all, and neither of us pretended that we did.

I decided that I had nothing to lose in trying to get the fight over the center stopped.

So, I agreed that I would try—but I offered no guarantees.

I told her that I'd let her know what I found out and that she needed to get the word out beforehand to stop her side from doing anything while I tried to locate the leadership of Doggden, if there was any.

She said that she'd already made the calls and that everything had stopped; this was a surprising admission to me, that she had that kind of control and that the family was indeed in charge of South Side 18th Street.

I spent the next two days talking to anyone that would listen, trying to get the word out that I was looking for someone—anyone really—who had leadership in the Doggden Gang.

Then one day I found a very cryptic message on my voicemail.

I was told to talk to a woman in an apartment in the inner city; the message left on my office phone named an address and an apartment number, and it said to contact her about the shootings at the center.

I went to the apartment, and after verbally dancing around for about a half an hour she finally came to the point.

"I understand you want to talk about the shootings at the center?"

She hadn't admitted anything, but her eye contact and nonverbal communication said a lot.

She was talking about the truce that I'd been asking around about on the street.

I told her that I'd been asked to communicate a request for a truce and that South Side 18th Street would withdraw from the center if the shooting stopped.

I told her that I had a guarantee from their leadership that this would occur; they simply wanted the shooting to end.

She argued that they'd started the fight and that the "muthafuckin hood had responded."

I agreed and told her that they hadn't anticipated the reaction that they'd received.

The center wasn't worth the fight to the 18th Street gang; they wanted a truce.

She said that she couldn't promise anything, but she'd talk to some people and see what she could do; she was a spokesperson, not a leader.

I saw inside the dark apartment that there were several large black males milling around, anxious and listening to the conversation; so, I made it clear that I'd been approached by South Side 18th Street and asked to deliver the message, and that I felt that they were serious.

I told her that I needed an answer that day, but she said that she couldn't give me one.

I pushed the point, saying that I needed an answer from whoever would make that decision that day and that I'd wait 'til I got one.

If the group of men in the house didn't want me to find out who they were, they'd be trapped there—and I was hoping that that alone would be enough to push a decision.

I waited thirty minutes outside the house, nervous as hell that at any moment they'd get tired of this candy ass shit and come out of the house shooting.

Arms crossed and leaning against my car, I tried to look relaxed; however, my hand was on my Glock in my shoulder holster the entire time, unsnapped and ready to go.

Finally, she came out and walked up to me and said, "It's done, motherfucker—but you better be for real, or your ass is in deep shit! One black brother gets a cap in his ass, and we'll come for you first, motherfucker, then we'll go after the Mexicans."

Laughing, I said, "OK, I'll deliver the message." *(Laughing is what I do when I'm starting to get angry.)*

I then gave her my card and said, "If you have any more problems, call me, and I'll take care of it myself."

I left and went directly to the Gardenas' home, telling the mother of the family about the exchange.

I made it clear that if anything happened at the center, I'd hold her personally responsible and target her anyway I could.

I knew that she worked for a local Mexican restaurant and that if the owner found out who she really was, he'd fire her.

I also made it clear that, if she was lying to me, I'd do anything I could to destroy her and her entire family.

She just closed the door.

A week went by, and nothing happened at the center; life returned to normal.

I checked the center frequently, looking for South Side 18th Street graffiti or gang members, but there were none.

The shootings stopped, and both sides kept their word.

I was amazed.

Had I really just negotiated a truce between two street gangs?

No one would believe this shit; I barely did myself.

The street was always very educational...and unpredictable.

"LEVI" AND EME

I WAS ALWAYS REALLY INTERESTED in taggers and had spent a lot of time collecting pictures of tags done by artists in the city.

One tagger in particular became a frequent contact, and I developed an uneasy relationship with him over a period of several years.

I'd noticed a pattern that most every tagger developed: they liked to tag either near their house, or somewhere they'd see the work that they'd done on a very frequent basis.

Taggers are very proud of their work and see themselves as street artists, and some *are* very talented.

They have a very different motivation than the usual gang member, although they can morph quickly into a gang if they're threatened as a group.

This particular tagger was a scribe, or a writer. He had some artistic ability and did do some murals on buildings and walls, but his passion was tagging his moniker all over the city.

He'd done a couple murals near his house, and I took a wild guess that he was the tagger "Levi" who had written the tags and murals.

I approached him on it, and initially he denied it.

He had quite a reputation with the cops and didn't trust any of us *(not that I could blame him)*, so it took several months to gain his limited trust.

I kept at it, though, and eventually one day I was driving past and he came out of his house and waved me down.

He started off with small talk, then he got to the point.

He said, "Hypothetically speaking, if I was 'Levi', what would you wanna talk about?"

I told him that I was interested in tags and the process that went into making a mural, as well as why the tagger chose the moniker; honestly, the whole subculture was an interest to me.

There are taggers worldwide, in every culture and nation, and they range in age from little kids to older grownups.

There are also tagger magazines, publications, and websites.

He listened and watched me for several minutes, then said, "I may be able to help you learn a thing or two, but I'm not this 'Levi' person— what did you call him, a tagger?"

A big smile grew across his face, then he said, "Come back in a couple days, and maybe we'll talk."

Another example of how listening to what *isn't* being said is more important than what *is* being said.

I returned a few days later, and we did talk.

I got to know him and his family really well.

He dated the daughter of one of the SPPD records clerks, and they had a baby together; the clerk hated him with a passion, though, and I had to agree never to talk to her about him or share anything I learned about him with her.

He said that he just wanted to get along with her as well as he possibly could and didn't want to cause problems.

I'd talked to the clerk on several occasions, and she admitted to being a female gang member in California and always carried a knife.

She bragged about stabbing two Black guys who had tried to rape her when she lived in California and claimed that she was a member of Sur 13.

She'd earned the nickname "Mad Dog" in the police department because she was one crazy bitch.

She was one of the brass's favorites and had a lot of pull with the senior members of the administration through three Police Chiefs' administrations.

As time went on, the tagger admitted that he was, in fact, "Levi," and he began to trust me on a limited basis.

He was frequently arrested for various minor things, and each time he was locked up, I had to start over rebuilding his trust.

One night I stopped by his house, and he was installing hydraulics in a car.

He had a reputation on the street for being able to install the hydraulics exceptionally well, and gang members from several different sets would pay him to do work on their cars.

He sat down and explained the install process to me one night, going into great detail about what was required to make the cars do what he wanted them to do. It was really an education; he was quite skilled.

He told me about several cars he'd done for different guys in the city. I'd seen a few of them, and they were very impressive.

I returned a few days later and found him depressed.

His girl had broken up with him and taken their son, and he was angry.

He asked me if I knew what the EME was.

I replied that I did; they're the Mexican mafia.

He said that he knew of a certain records clerk at a Police Dept. who had been living with a Mexican Mafia member for many years.

He said that the clerk bragged about how she'd manipulated the senior administration of the police department for years and had them fooled thinking that she could be trusted.

She bragged about how she'd provided her boyfriend with information on drug dealers and arrests that the police had made, who the police informants were, and how they worked cases.

I asked him why he was telling me this now, and he said that a certain records clerk had talked her daughter into leaving him and taking their son—and he was pissed off.

I then told him about all that I'd found out about how the jail, the juvenile correctional system, and the cops had been infiltrated, saying that I really doubted I could do much with this information to help him out; no one ever believed me, even when I showed them proof.

He was drinking beer and stopped talking for a few minutes.

He then looked up at me and said, "Doesn't that bother you that you know all this stuff and no one listens?"

I said it did but that I'd found out that most cops were really stupid about the street and were more concerned with their egos, thinking they knew what was going on instead of really learning the streets.

The brass was also to blame for this stupidity; they "encouraged" (*"demanded" was more like it*) ticket writing to increase the city government's revenues—which damaged our relationships with the people in the street; no one liked the unofficial tax that writing tickets really was.

I left that night and wondered about what he'd told me.

Meanwhile, the clerk he was talking about quit the department less than a week later and left without notice; she just disappeared.

I asked him about it, and he said, "Maybe a certain records clerk found out a certain detective knew her secret?"

I never confirmed what he told me—but I did believe it. We had huge leaks of information within the department.

Narcotics would get ready to do a bust, and twenty minutes before they'd hit a house the occupants would vacate the building, running to cars and leaving the area.

Informants would be found out, and entire blocks of information on certain people would disappear from the computer databases...*someone* was doing that stuff.

I had informants telling me that someone in the Narcotics Strike Force was trading information for money and drugs.

Girls who worked the streets constantly told me stories of cops who had traded them being arrested for sexual favors, and in some cases cocaine for painkillers.

I was getting really jaded.

I didn't trust anyone that I worked with, and no one in the system seemed legit.

I trusted my own informants more than any cop I worked with; at the very least, I knew that I could prove they were honest, and I felt I knew what their agenda was about.

CRAZED NEGOTIATOR

AFTER THE DRIVE-BY AT OSO'S house, the armed confrontation at Speedy's house, and the truce negotiated at the Fred Marshall Center between Doggden and South Side 18th Street, the Matriarch that led South Side 18th Street called me again and left a message on my cell phone.

She asked that I meet her at their new place.

It was on a short, out of the way street that had been having frequent drive-by shootings the past few weeks.

There would be reports of shots fired and people screaming, but when we showed up there would be nothing but silence...dead silence.

She asked that I come to the house after work.

She still worked at a local popular Mexican restaurant and would be home about 12:30 or 1 a.m.

I arrived early and watched the house.

The conversation I had with the West Side 18th Street set was still fresh in my mind, and although they'd been nowhere near me, I didn't believe for one second that the hit was called off; I thought they'd just wait 'til I relaxed, then try something.

So I watched and waited, but I saw nothing to make me more paranoid than I already was.

I idled in, lights out on my unmarked car, slowly rolling down the street, windows down, listening.

When I arrived at the address, I quietly got out of the car, gently pressed the door closed, then started to walk towards the house.

The mother of the family came out of the front door with her oldest daughter.

They began to talk to me, making small talk and asking about the rumors they'd heard about the West Side 18th Street meeting and my talk with them.

I ignored their questions, but they persisted.

The mother made a comment that she'd heard that I'd lost my fucking mind and had gone totally crazy.

She was looking at me, trying to size up my reaction.

She said word was out on the street that I'd gone crazy and was totally fucking loco.

The entire time, she was watching me, looking for a reaction; she just kept repeating the same thing over and over again in different ways, watching me for a reaction.

I said, "So why did you want me here? No way in hell you're concerned for my fuckin' welfare. So what the fuck do you want?"

She eventually cut to the chase and asked if I'd heard about all the shootings on their street the past few weeks.

I said that I had.

She said that there had been problems with the Nortaneos family that lived on the opposite end of the street; they didn't want a South Side 18th Street family on their street.

She said that when she moved into the house she didn't know that Nortaneos gang members lived on the street, and now she couldn't afford to move.

She then asked if I could talk to the family down the street for her.

This was getting really weird.

I didn't expect more negotiations.

I was worried about being set up, watching my back constantly with the bangers on the streets and the cops I worked with.

Detectives are intensely competitive, and I'd made even more enemies with my success on the recent cases, in spite of the interference by my fellow gang detectives.

I explained to the woman that my only contact with the Nortaneos hadn't been positive.

I had no rapport with them as a group. They weren't like the rest of the gangs in St. Pauls; being outnumbered, they were very suspicious and just wanted to be left alone.

I explained that after I'd showed up at the wedding, looking for Pedro Lechuga about a year and a half earlier, on the Snoopy shooting, they hadn't warmed up to me at all.

While I was explaining this to her, a car came around the corner at the opposite end of the street.

We were standing by my unmarked car in the street, away from a nearby streetlight; basically, all three of us were talking in the dark when the car came around the corner and turned its lights out.

The car quietly rolled to a stop, and I could hear it idling; it was late and dark, and the sound of the engine carried to where we were.

The woman I'd been talking to asked her daughter, "Who is that? Do you recognize the car?"

The daughter was also as deep in the gang culture as you could possibly be. *(Gangbangers pay serious attention to the cars and people around them; their situational awareness is much higher than the average person.)*

She was pregnant with the child of a subordinate Lt. in the gang and knew as much as any member did, possibly more.

They watched for a minute, and when the windows rolled down on our side of the street they cried out in a panic and ran towards their house, screaming, "Get the fuck down! They're gonna do a drive-by on us!"

I didn't move.

The woman ran behind the house, and the daughter ran inside.

They were both large women who slowly ambled when they walked.

It wasn't easy to move all that body weight; their usual gait reminded me of elephants at the zoo, rockin' back and forth and taking a step every now and then as they breathed loudly—and talked even louder—their huge breasts resting on huge folds of fat, which rested on even more folds of fat.

They were very large women; however, when the windows rolled down on the mystery car and they realized that they were about to get shot at—all that sloth began to move with a purpose.

They were amazingly fast, crossing the front yard and flying up the stairs and into the house in a few short seconds.

Left alone in the front yard, I watched the car and realized that they still hadn't seen us, nor had they seen the women's rapid escape.

I could see movement in the car, though, and that arms were coming out of the open windows.

I had another huge adrenaline dump.

As I pulled my gun from the shoulder holster, I heard the mother yelling to me, "Pacman, get the fuck outta the street! You're gonna get killed!"

I still wasn't sure that she hadn't set me up.

I thought I'd watched the house long enough and was processing in my mind if I'd missed anything, anything in the conversation, their behavior—had they set me up?

I didn't know for sure.

Regardless, I was here.

The car was here.

The windows were down—and it was painfully obvious what was about to happen.

I pulled out an extra clip from the shoulder holster and held it so I could do a combat reload when the shooting started.

I then stepped into the streetlights.

I was really calm, but very intensely pissed off as well; this shit was starting to piss me off.

I was *never* gonna run from this shit.

I wasn't gonna go through another high-speed chase or be worried about being ambushed.

Whoever it was, if they wanted a fight—I was gonna make it really easy for them.

I was armed and I was gonna kill as many of them as I could.

As I waited in the street, there was movement inside the car that sat at the opposite end; windows down, an occasional gun coming out of a window, then going back inside the car.

I started to get more pissed off and yelled out, challenging them and holding up my arms in typical gangbanger fashion—gun in the right hand, spare clip in the left—screaming, "Come on, bitches! Let's *do* this!"

We had a standoff there for what seemed like a very long time; it was probably only seconds, but it seemed like forever.

The car finally shifted into reverse and slowly backed up, lights still out, then pulled away.

I waited for them to come back, expecting them to return from another direction at any moment to finish the drive-by; they never came back, though.

Eventually, the women came back from the house.

The mother was laughing and crying at the same time.

The slow ambling gait had returned, and they were still breathing hard from the rapid sprint across the front lawn.

They called me a "fuckin' lunatic" and said that they "had never seen some shit like that."

I was barely listening.

Still in a rage, adrenaline still flowing—and still not convinced that they hadn't set me up—I got in my car and left them standing there.

I don't know what became of them after that...I never saw them again.

LAST GASP

MY LAST ATTEMPT TO GET the administration at the department to listen and deal with the gang problem proactively—and not reactively—was over some gang graffiti I found in a city park.

I was driving around, looking for new graffiti, and I got out and checked a restroom at the park.

I found a bunch of gang graffiti there that was for a gang I'd never heard of before; it appeared to be gang graffiti mixed with satanic symbols.

I had no idea who they were and had never heard of them, so I took a few pictures and went back to the office to decipher them.

I found the graffiti to be a Sureneos gang that went by "MS" and "Mara Salvatrucha 13."

I'd never heard of them, so I asked if anyone spoke more fluent Spanish than I did—and everyone referred me to Maria, the Major Crimes Detectives' secretary.

She and I didn't get along, though, and I didn't want to go to her for help of any kind.

So, I looked for a few days for anyone else who might help, but no one had heard of the group on the street, and none of the people I knew who spoke Spanish knew what the words meant.

I'd called a contact that I'd developed in the Los Angeles CRASH unit to ask if he knew about the gang, but I hadn't heard back from him.

Finally, as a last resort, I asked Maria if she knew what the word meant.

She looked at them and said, "Trucha is 'trout' in Spanish."

She looked at it a minute longer, then said, "I think that what you think is gang graffiti is really some trout fisherman!"

She laughed and laughed, making a point of telling everyone that some guy that had been writing about his fishing trip on the bathroom walls had duped me.

Jesus, she was an annoying fucking bitch; I really hated her.

The problem again, though, was that she also had the ears of the brass and went so far as to tell them that I was stupid and paranoid and had been duped by the "trout fisherman."

Finally, my friend in the Los Angeles CRASH unit called me back.

I told him about the MS13 graffiti, and he said that they were one of the most violent gangs in the United States.

They had their roots in the El Salvadorian revolution, and they weren't only Sur 13 gang members—they believed in satanic worship as well. *(That fit the graffiti I found.)*

He recommended that I get a hold of my administration immediately and make them aware that we had this particular gang in the area.

He said that they made 18th Street look like little kids in the park playing baseball by comparison.

I thanked him for his help and hung up.

I then wrote up a memo and sent it up the chain to the brass.

I don't know how far it got, but I got it back a few days later with a yellow sticky note on it that said, "We don't have the time or the resources to investigate trout fishing."

It wasn't signed.

I'd received it through the department interoffice mail, so it had at least gone to the Assistant Chief.

After that, I turned in my resignation from the gang unit, asking for a transfer back to patrol.

The Sergeant called me into his office, asked me to close the door, then proceeded to rake me over the coals.

How dare I desert the unit and him?

He'd counted on me to carry the unit and had structured it around my continued presence.

He said I needed to think about more than myself—what would the rest of the officers in the unit do without my help?

I plainly said that that wasn't my problem.

My two years was up, and I wasn't going out on the department's terms; I'd leave on my own terms.

I'd set a timetable, and I intended to keep it.

I'd learned why it was so hard to be successful in the unit: it was structured to fail.

Just like in my childhood, though, I succeeded in spite of my surroundings.

The feeling was all too familiar; it was time to read the writing on the wall: time to go.

I left gangs a short time later.

I was fried, burned out, and paranoid, and I didn't trust anyone I worked with anymore.

I continued to be called upon to help out with cases that involved gang members, but only as a last resort.

I was seen as an outsider; when the detectives had no other option, they'd ask for help.

JOKER GETS LOST, THEN FOUND

I WORKED SECURITY PART-TIME AT a department store for six years.

I got to know a lot of people there, one of whom was Dan Sears.

He worked in the men's clothing area, and when it was slow he'd ask me questions about what it was like to be a cop.

He'd always end the conversation with the comment that he was glad he wasn't a cop because he didn't think he'd want to be exposed to that life.

I told him that it was my opinion that you couldn't hide from "that life"; I thought it was better to be aware of it than ignorant of it.

He disagreed.

He was very religious and felt that as long as he lived by the teachings of his church, he'd be protected; he had no need to learn of any other life.

One day I went to work, and he wasn't there, so I asked around about him; I thought that he'd probably quit because the store had an extremely high turnover rate.

The girls that I asked, though, said that he hadn't quit.

They then looked at each other quietly—their eye contact speaking volumes—and one asked me, "Didn't you hear the news?"

I said, "No, what news?"

"He was killed by a group of gang members on the street near his house. They stabbed him in a fight."

I didn't know where he lived, so I looked into it.

Turns out, he lived near my house *(I'd just divorced my second wife and had been forced by finances to move into the city)* and had, in fact, been stabbed by gang members as he sat in his car.

I was working in schools at the time and was glad I wouldn't have to work that case.

A few months went by, and I'd tried to forget about the stabbing.

I had to check in with my boss at the time, and I'd stop by Detectives to see what was new with the few people left that I liked in the department.

On this day in particular, I overheard the Lead Detective assigned to the Sears case asking his Lieutenant if he could ask "someone" for help.

The detective said that he'd talked to everyone he knew and asked everyone he could for help, but he couldn't find this last guy involved in the murder of Sears.

The last guy that he couldn't find had gone deep; he'd been the killer and had to most to lose.

He said, "You know I don't wanna ask him for help, but if we're gonna get this last guy, I have to try."

The Lt. was Leeds, and he and I didn't get along at all.

The Lead Detective was Skidmark, and we didn't get along at all either.

Leeds yelled at Skidmark, "I don't fuckin' like this! You know I don't like him! If you get any information, you keep it quiet. We can solve our cases without his help. This is bullshit! He won't find him anyway—and if he does, you don't tell anyone he helped, you understand me? You tell no one!"

Skidmark said that he did understand, then left Leeds' office.

As he came out, he looked around and saw me, and his shoulders dropped; it was then that I realized they were talking about me.

I smiled, turned around laughing, and left Detectives.

That night, Skidmark called me at home and asked for my help.

He said, "I know you overheard the conversation in Leeds' office, but I need your help. I'm looking for Joker from the SP Treces. Do you know him?"

"Don't insult me," I replied. "Of course, I fuckin' know him. What did he do?"

Skidmark said that he was the killer of Dan Sears, that he stabbed Sears in the chest while Sears sat in his car and asked Joker and his friends not to talk to his girlfriend.

Turns out that Joker and company had talked some trash to Sears' girlfriend.

He'd just left to go to the store or something, and while he was gone they walked by his house and said some sexually explicit remarks to his girl.

When he returned, she told him, and he felt it was his duty to ask them not to talk to his girl that way.

This was the way Sears was: honorable, but naïve.

Anyway, so they stabbed him in his chest in the car.

Skidmark wanted me to help him, and Leeds was pissed that he even had to ask for my help.

Skidmark even had the balls to ask me to give him information on my informants.

I laughed; there was no way that was ever gonna happen.

I had an understanding with them that I *never* disclosed who gave me information—no matter what—and I made it really clear to him that he'd never get that information, ever.

If he wanted my help, I'd ask around, and if I got information on Joker he'd have to guarantee me that no matter what time of the day or night, he'd come.

If he couldn't make that promise, then I wouldn't help him.

He agreed and said that he could pay my informant if they produced.

I told him that they all worked for free, but that if he wanted to give me money to pass along, I'd do it after the fact; no one who worked for me worked for money.

Skidmark wasn't comfortable with this, but he agreed.

He wanted control of everything—but that was too fucking bad.

I called my most dependable informant in the gang involved, SP-13, and asked what they knew about Joker, such as where he'd been or if he was still in town.

The informant asked why I wanted to know, and I told them about the stabbing and what had happened—AND that SPPD's finest couldn't find him anywhere and the detectives needed the help of "two fucked up wannabe thugs like us to get this dude."

He laughed, and we exchanged insults about who the wannabe really was.

Finally, he agreed to ask around and see what he could find out. I never had any doubt that he'd ask around; he loved the fact that he could make a difference in the city and outperform "the man" *(cops)* when it came to hunting down bad guys.

I told him to call day or night, which was our standard practice; whenever I asked for a favor, it was always big and always 24/7.

He knew that I'd never give him up.

Two days later at 10:30 pm, I got a call.

My informant said that Joker was in an apartment in Central City.

He'd been there for several weeks without leaving, and he said that he knew for sure that he was there now—but he didn't know for how much longer.

I wrote down the address, then called Skidmark at home.

He was reluctant, complaining that it was late and he was tired.

I said, "Look, motherfucker, you wanted this dude—he's there now. I'm on my way, and this isn't my fuckin' case, so get off your fuckin' ass and get in here—or I'll arrest him myself and let Leeds know you had a shot at him and didn't take it."

He changed his mind quickly and got on his way.

We coordinated deployment prior to arrival: I took the back door, Skidmark took the front.

In typical Skidmark fashion, he tried to bully his way in rather than talk his way in, accompanied by a patrol unit; I was alone in the back, listening and thinking to myself that some people will never learn.

Then the back door opened up—and there was Joker.

He stepped out of the apartment and slowly walked down the stairs.

Hidden in the shadows with my gun pointed at his head, I spoke up and said, "'Sup, Joker?"

He turned to me and said, "'Sup, Pacman?"

"Not a thing," I said. "Just out to get some fresh air."

He says, "Ya, it's nice tonight."

I said "So? What's it gonna be? You tired of running? We gonna fight, or do we do this like men?"

He said, "Ya, I am tired of running."

I asked him to turn around, then I cuffed him.

No fight, and no disrespect; it was over.

I told him that Skidmark was upfront and that he (*Joker*) gave him a run for his money, "but in the end the motherfucker had to come to me to find you, so you keep your head up. You didn't go down like a bitch."

He said, "Alright. Thanks, man."

We walked to the front of the apartment where Skidmark was still trying to bully his way in, and I turned Joker over to him.

He said thanks to me, then immediately started in on the guy about what a piece of shit he was.

I went home and called my informant.

He had a perfect record for finds and information, and I gave them feedback on what happened, every detail and every word.

I also mentioned that they might get some money this time, if he was interested; he was, so I passed the money along.

The next time I saw Lt. Leeds, he wouldn't even look at me; the mutual dislike continued to grow between us.

No one ever knew that I found and arrested Joker—with a lot of help from a really good informant.

THE ALEX MASCARENAS' HOMICIDE

I NEEDED TO BE OFF the streets, so I volunteered to go to schools; I saw that as a way to unwind a little bit and hopefully get out of the street mentality.

I'd been in schools about a year when I got a phone call and was told to go to the Major Crimes unit; they had a case involving a child who had been shot in the park in Central City in the middle of the day.

The shooting appeared to be gang related, but the scene was confusing; they couldn't tell what had happened or why.

The entire case was confusing; there were several things that had gone on simultaneously, and they needed any help that I could provide with the interviews of the kids involved.

I was originally brought in because the victim was in my school.

I didn't know him at all; he was a Special Ed kid, and I'd seen him in the halls but had spent no time with him.

He'd been sitting with his family, watching a baseball game in the park, and had been shot in the head for no apparent reason.

He died in his mother's arms.

The investigation revealed that there had been a fight between St. Pauls 13 and South Side 18th Street at the park about a half an hour earlier.

The fight was over, and patrols had stopped several kids in the area and FI'ed *(field interviewed)* them.

The kids had then gone on their way when the cops were done.

Then another fight had broken out about two blocks south of the park; this fight involved adults and a car.

The occupants had fled the area, though, so even though the neighbors had called the fight in, by the time cops arrived the fight was over and everyone was gone.

Shots had been fired in the fight, and it appeared to detectives that one of the shots had missed its target and traveled two blocks up the street and hit the victim, Alex Mascarenas, in the head—killing him instantly.

I didn't want to be involved in this case in any way, shape, or form; nonetheless, I was brought in as a possible link to the first fight that had occurred.

Some of the kids in my school had been in that fight, so I went to talk to them.

Riqo Luna was one of the kids involved in the fight, as well as the Ortiz brothers, Andrew and Joseph.

I spoke to all of them, and I remember that Luna was really shaken up by the shooting.

He knew who Alex Mascarenas was and had liked him; his death hit Luna hard.

I talked to him for some time but he had nothing to offer me about the shooting.

So, I spent some time trying to help him cope with the bad news rather than gathering anything meaningful to help in the investigation.

I returned to the police station and briefed the lead detective—Skidmark again *(lucky me)*—on what I'd learned, which wasn't much.

The two incidents appeared to be unrelated.

Skidmark told me that he thought the shooting was gang related.

He said that several witnesses saw that there was a car driving around in the area of the 38 and 3900 block of Ellis.

The car had four occupants, and a woman was driving.

There was also a Black dude in the front seat, and they'd been trying to start a beef with South Side 18th Street gang members in the area.

They were there looking for a fight, coming back time and time again and calling out "St. Pauls 13!", trying to get the 18th Street gang members to come out and fight them.

I told them that the only Black gang member in St. Pauls 13 that I knew of that wasn't locked up in prison was Doughboy.

I had a really good rapport with Doughboy and had talked to him many times over the years.

I'd handled the shooting in which he'd been shot in the ass several years earlier.

So, I volunteered to locate Doughboy and interview him.

At the time I volunteered, I really hoped that I would have been refused.

I didn't want any part of this case, or working with anyone in Detectives; I knew how notoriously sloppy they were when it came to protecting informants and keeping their mouths shut about cases.

Unfortunately, I was asked to locate and interview Doughboy, if he would talk to me.

So, I picked up Doughboy's last known address from the department's database and started there.

After a series of contacts, I eventually ended up at his mother's house in Widefield.

I'd met her several times over the years I'd spent at SPPD, and she invited me in and asked me what had happened this time.

I told her that I didn't know if he was involved or not but that it had to do with the boy that was shot in the park.

She started to cry; the years of his gang life had taken their toll on her.

She'd been contacted numerous times in his short life for fights and stabbings and his being shot, and now she wondered if her son had murdered this young boy.

She was really upset.

She told me that he wasn't home but when he did come home, she'd call me.

I told her to remind him of who I was; he knew me, and we'd been on good terms.

She said that she would and that she remembered me as well, then thanked me for trying to help her son over the years.

She did say, however, that she felt he was beyond help.

I left the house, and a few hours later I got a call from Doughboy's mom, telling me that he was home.

I went and picked him up and asked him what had happened, and he gave me the basics.

He said that they'd been driving around the area, looking for "sewer rats". *(South Side 18th Street gang members.)*

He was the passenger in the front of the car, they'd been drinking, and they'd decided to go pick a fight with any random 18th Street gang member they could find.

They ended up in Central City, yelling out challenges to anyone they thought might be 18th street—and that's when a guy had come out of his house on the west side of the street with a rifle.

Doughboy jumped out of the car and "called the guy's bluff"; he didn't believe that he'd shoot him with a rifle. *(It was amazing to me that Doughboy hadn't learned from the first shooting.)*

The South Side 18th Street guy shot at Doughboy, then at the car as he jumped in and they took off to get away.

Doughboy said that his group hadn't fired a shot.

I tried to get him to give me statement about the incident, and he nearly did and started to write it out.

Then he stopped and said, "No, I can't. I'm going to prison; I know it, and you know it—and I can't go as a snitch."

I had to respect that.

He'd at least given me a start: he'd admitted to being there and had confirmed witness accounts of the fight.

Detective work is a series of steps.

Doughboy had given me much, and at that point a lot of detectives would call their witness names or belittle them; I never did this.

Anything they said was better than nothing, and in my mind even an outright lie at least told me what did *not* happen.

Doughboy had a warrant and was definitely gonna be locked up, but I let it go and just talked to him.

I asked him how he'd been and how his ass had healed from the shooting years earlier.

He laughed about that; we both did.

Then I took him to the jail and booked him.

As we walked in, he passed an inmate being released.

He told the guy to call him and yelled out a local phone number.

I pretended not to pay attention, but I memorized the number and wrote it down when he wasn't looking.

He knew he was gonna be locked up a long time, and he wouldn't get any phone calls—so the number he was giving out was most likely someone who had been in the car, letting them know that he'd been locked up; it was a warning to his gang that we, the police, were onto them.

I left the jail, then got on my cell phone immediately to dispatch and had them look up the address associated with the phone number; it belonged to a woman who lived in West St. Pauls.

I went to the house and found that no one was home.

There was mail in the mailbox near the door, so I pulled it out to see what was there.

There were bills, ads, and a letter from Doughboy to the occupant, a woman *(I thought most likely a girlfriend)*.

The driver of the car involved in the incident had been a woman, and I was hopeful that this was her.

I had dispatch search the address and the girl's name for previous cases, but we had very little on the occupant or the address.

So, I parked a few blocks away for a while and watched the house; nothing happened.

Feeling hungry and needing a break, I went to get something to eat, then returned.

When I did, a woman was in the yard feeding her dogs, pit bull puppies.

I took off my gun and badge, got out of my car, then walked up and approached her.

As I started talking about the dogs, she was noticeably nervous; she talked to me, but she watched me carefully.

I said to her, "I'm not gonna bullshit you; I'm a cop, a detective with the city—but I'm also a friend of Doughboy's. He sent me out here to talk to you."

She asked about him and what had happened to him, and I told her that he was locked up for a warrant and that he'd asked me to come and tell her just that; he'd told me that she meant a lot to him and that he wanted her to know what happened.

I told her that Doughboy had said that he couldn't be a snitch but had asked that I talk to her and that maybe she could help me out. *(This was all a lie.)*

She was quiet for a long time and just petted the dogs.

Finally, she turned to me and asked, "What do you wanna know?"

I asked her what had happened, and she told me the same story that he had—only she included who was in the car, their names, and the fact that they were her cousins.

They were also previously undocumented St. Pauls 13 gang members, and I didn't know them at all.

When I asked about the car and where it was, she said, "In the garage behind you."

I asked her to show me, and she did.

It was the car that they'd used to escape the gunfight.

I asked her to give me a written statement detailing all that had happened, and she agreed to do so.

She did, however, want to take care of her dogs first.

I agreed that it would be no problem and told her that I'd wait for her in my car.

While I waited, I called Skidmark and told him the names that she'd given me.

I also told him where the car they'd driven was located and that she'd agreed to give me a statement.

I said that we'd be on our way to the police station in a few minutes and asked him to wait 'til I had her there at the station before he went to pick up the other two occupants of the car.

I explained *(very slowly, using small words)* that we needed her statement; she controlled the car and had the most control over where they'd been and what they had done.

I did get her statement, and she outlined everything that had happened; she was very cooperative.

When I gave Skidmark the statement—in typical Skidmark (*stupid motherfucker*) fashion, he read it, then started in on her.

He called her a "piece of shit" and told her that she was responsible for the death of Mascarenas; he didn't have the case locked up by any stretch of the imagination, yet he was already alienating his witnesses.

Jesus, this was frustrating.

I wanted no part of this stupid shit.

No way would Skidmark ever close this case with an arrest doing this stupid shit; it was a long time before he'd ever be in court, and the case was a long way from him being able to make an arrest of the suspect.

I left the station, leaving him to his "police work."

Before my help, they didn't have a thing, but I was able to get him all the people in the car identified, the location of the car itself, and statements from the suspects and witnesses—just by talking to people and treating them with respect.

Skidmark couldn't understand that gang cases are a process of gaining trust and that you have to treat your witnesses and suspects with respect or you'll never get a successful prosecution.

The case never made it to the inside of a courtroom; the suspect fled to Mexico, and the witnesses refused to cooperate.

Once again, my assistance was minimized to the brass, so I wrote a very short supplemental report and was done helping with this incredibly fucked up case.

TRANSFORMATION

TO GIVE YOU AN IDEA about how jaded and angry I'd become, here are a couple great examples of how I'd changed.

From the green rookie "Can I help you, poor citizen who has lost your way?" in Chapter 6 of *CurbChek* to this:

After I returned to patrol and had been through the shootings, I was an FTO *(field training officer)*.

I was tasked with teaching new officers how to complete paperwork, write reports that would get convictions, and try to teach them the street.

One day, I was driving around in Central City; actually, I was the passenger, the trainee was driving.

I looked over into the car next to us and saw Adam Medina.

He was an SPVG gang member, and his brother, Johnny Medina, was an SPVG gang member as well; the whole gang lifestyle permeated their family.

Several gang bangers had told me that Adam Medina was looking for me, meaning that he wanted to shoot me and was putting out the word to the rest of the gang members that he was "gonna put a bullet in my ass."

I'd also heard from one of the guys in the gang unit that they'd been told the same thing.

Medina had been talking a lot of shit on the street, saying how he was gonna "bust some caps in my ass."

I didn't know what the reason was that he'd suddenly taken an interest in me; I'd been out of gangs for some time.

Apparently he had though, and there I was looking over at him in the car next to me.

I told the guy I was training, "That's Adam Medina next to us."

I kept watching, and it appeared to me that he'd seen me as well and that he was looking down at something in his hands; it looked like he was manipulating whatever was in his hands while pretending to be unaware of my presence.

I started to get pissed off.

I thought he had a gun that he was preparing to shoot me with, and if the fucker wanted to shoot me—I was *not* gonna be ambushed.

I told the trainee to pull in front of the car and pull it over.

He said, "What"?

I said, "Pull the fuck over *now*, goddamn it! Right fucking *now*!"

He looked at me like I was fucking nuts, but he did what I told him.

I then jumped out of the patrol car, gun out and pointed at the passenger of the car we'd stopped, and yelled at the guy in the car that I thought was Medina, "What now, motherfucker? What you got to say to me now?"

Then I told him to "get the fuck outta the car," pulled open his car door, and pulled him from the car; it was then that I noticed that he had a cell phone in his hand—not a gun.

I slammed him against the side of the car, my left hand on his throat and my right hand holding my Glock to the side of his head.

I said, "What now, bitch? You want me dead? Here the fuck I am! Go ahead, bitch—show me what you got!"

I wanted to kill him right there on the spot.

I didn't want to be ambushed like I'd seen so many gangbangers do, sneak up and shoot an enemy while they aren't looking; I wanted to make damn sure they fucking knew that if they came after me, I'd fight them and kill them—not thinking twice about it; so I was in this guy's face, hating his ass, wanting to kill him.

There I was in Central City in the middle of the day on a Saturday, seriously thinking about blowing his brains out.

Just then, I heard a voice that most definitely was *not* a gang banger's say, "Sir, I'm sorry for anything I've done. I don't know what I did, but I'm sorry."

There was real fear in that voice; no anger, nothing that sounded even remotely streetwise.

Everything slowed way down.

The sound of the street disappeared, and everything became quiet, like the way it sounds in the middle of a forest when the snow is falling: not just quiet, but sounds seemed to disappear.

I looked at who I thought was Adam Medina, and his face morphed in front of me: he was *not* Adam Medina; he looked nothing like Adam.

I had pulled some kid out of his car, gun to his head, and held him by the throat and scared the shit out of him—ready to kill his ass for nothing.

He had a cell phone and was driving next to me; that was all he'd done.

He didn't look or act like Medina in the slightest.

I released him and apologized, telling him that I thought he was someone else and that I was wrong.

I got back in the patrol car and told the trainee to get us the fuck out of there.

I thought about everything long and hard, the way I'd seen what I'd seen, the way the guy's face changed when he spoke from what I thought I saw to what he really looked like.

I was really fucked up; dangerously so.

I didn't know if this was what a flashback was like or if was I just losing my mind—but either way I'd nearly killed a guy for nothing.

I needed to get off the street before I hurt someone.

PERMANENTLY CHANGED

ANOTHER INCIDENT OUTSIDE OF THE department occurred at home.

I lived in a rural area; I'd moved my kids there to protect them from the shit I'd seen in the street.

I didn't want my children to grow up like I had and like I was seeing these kids growing up.

I felt somewhat safe at home; my guard was dropped.

I was walking down the hallway of our house, and my daughter was in the bathroom.

I looked in and watched her for a moment.

At the time, she was the single most amazing thing in my life.

She meant the world to me; now, we can barely speak to each other civilly.

I was watching her through the crack in the door as she pulled her hair up, doing the hairstyle changes that girls do, seeing how different styles look.

Then she put her fingers up to her chest.

She had two fingers on the right hand pointed out and one on the left, elbows out, looking in the mirror.

I was enraged instantly: my baby girl was throwing up gang signs for "2-1", the latest gang in St. Pauls, another transplant gang from California.

In spite of all that I'd done to try to protect my children, my worst fears had come true.

She was hiding that she was in a gang and was practicing throwing up signs in our fucking bathroom mirror.

As ridiculous as this fear sounds, I'd handled cases where girls younger than my daughter had been gang raped by their own choice as an initiation into the gang.

I'd talked with several parents who were lost as to what to do to get their kids out of the gang—and their children were younger than my daughter.

I burst through the door and said, "What the fuck are you doing?!"

She said, "Nothing," then dropped her hands.

I went off, cursing and swearing.

I told her that I wasn't stupid and that I knew what the fuck she was doing.

I was the sworn enemy of *every* gangbanger in St. Pauls and I would *not* have this shit in my house.

I said, "If you think you can bring that shit into our house and get it past me—you are fuckin' wrong. I will be in your *ass*! Don't lie to me! What the fuck were you doing?!"

She started to cry and said, "I was looking at nail polish in the mirror to see how it went with this shirt! I'm sorry!"

I grabbed her hands and looked: each finger had a different color.

I was shaking with rage and fear that my baby girl had become one of them.

I looked in her eyes, and I saw nothing there that was streetwise, hard, or defiant; instead, she was afraid of her father, scared of what I'd become.

I'd never be able to make this right.

I apologized and tried to explain, but I saw fear in her eyes when she looked at me.

I'd never talked to her like this; she was the most precious thing in my world.

I had two boys as well, but they were boys, rough and tumble, growling and wrestling.

She was my first child and more beautiful than anything I'd ever seen, and now I'd shown her a side of her father that she never should have seen—and I couldn't change that.

I hated what I'd needed to become to survive the job I worked.

A SPECIAL PREVIEW OF

CURBCHEK

RELOAD

ZACH FORTIER

WANNA GO FOR A RIDE?

FOR MOST COPS, A RIDE-ALONG is a pain in the ass.

You get some college or high school kid that has taken a course or two and is now an expert in the law enforcement.

Even worse, if your luck is really bad, you get the Criminal Justice major—the expert in all things law enforcement—commenting on your every traffic stop, every interview, evaluating your probable cause, and critiquing your abilities as a cop.

During my career, I had a few ride-alongs. Most were short-lived and moved on to friendlier, more patient officers. You get in my car and change the radio station, adjust the heater or air conditioner, then sit back and begin to critique my work—and you will find your ass on the side of the road in a bad part of town. If you're lucky, I *might* at least take you back to your car before telling you in no uncertain terms to get the hell out and don't bother coming back.

In my mind, the whole damn concept of a ride-along is flawed. It's the police department's idea of public relations. They require the ride-along to sign a waiver, releasing the department from liability should anything happen to them, and then they hop in the car. Smiling, shiny faces hoping to see some real action, have some "cop" experience to brag about to their classmates or friends.

Reality is, every night the cop goes out, he is armed, trained, and wearing body armor.

Every night, he is on guard the entire night, watching hands, eye contact, looking for weapons on every person he meets; listening not only to what every person he comes into contact with says, but how it is said, acutely aware of nonverbal communication; seeing potential threats everywhere.

The ride-along is a severe distraction, and another helpless person you're responsible for.

To make matters worse, they think they know everything and talk to everyone you meet. They never shut the hell up.

One night, a ride-along went out with one of the newer guys. The officer felt it was his duty to take the guy from one hot call to another.

They started out the shift hitting the first domestic that came in. A man and his wife had been drinking and fighting, and the man had beaten his wife up. The scene was secure, and by the time they arrived it was pretty much just a peep show, walking the ride-along through the scene and explaining what had happened.

The ride-along was disappointed; he wanted to see some "real action", not a cold domestic, but the situation was all cleaned up and the fighting was already over.

Next call was a DUI. The officer went to help out and stand by while the FSTs *(field sobriety tests)* were being done, and fill out the impound sheet for the suspect's car after it was towed.

This is the reality of cop work: boredom and paperwork, helping the other guy out, hoping to keep each other safe and prevent a situation from going bad and becoming a "CNN moment."

The ride-along complained that "this was boring" and he wanted to see some real action!!!

If it was me, he would have been out of the car at that point, walking his candy ass back to the police station, mumbling about what a prick I was as he passed the drunks and transients that frequented the area.

Police work isn't a ride in an amusement park; you pay a fee for fake thrills and the almost-danger of going fast on something that you have to be "this tall to ride."

This is the real deal, not a ride, and there's no safety inspector to warn you when things are getting ready to go to shit and ask you if you are sure you want to stay on the ride.

The night wore on with the cop trying to get his ride-along to more interesting calls, and the ride-along complaining that he was bored.

They were on another traffic stop that was a carload of gang bangers. They had stopped the car because it matched the description of a car involved in a drive by.

The incident had happened a few hours earlier, and they were checking out the occupants of the vehicle, getting identification on each and looking for weapons.

For the cops, it's a tense moment. Any traffic stop can go to shit in a moment, and that moment passes so fast, if you're not watching everything and seeing it almost before it happens, you end up breathing from new holes in your chest or face that aren't supposed to be there.

This stop was going well, and while they were identifying everyone, the ride-along sat in the car. Another unit stopped by, and they began to help out in the stop.

The cop had a weird feeling, he said later, and it turned out to be right.

The two officers re-approached the car and began to remove the occupants one at a time. Finally, they got down to just the driver and the right front passenger.

The officer that started the stop was talking to the driver, and the back up was on the passenger side, watching the front passenger.

While talking to the driver, the first cop was also watching the front passenger.

It's a reality of the job that you have to be aware of everything going on at all times; impossible task, but you try.

Anyway, while he was talking to the driver, the passenger looked back and saw the back up cop watching his every move.

What neither of the cops knew was that the carload of bangers had recently done a home burglary, and the trunk of the car was loaded up with rifles and handguns stolen in the burglary.

They had been driving around with the intention of "putting in work," meaning they were looking to get into a gunfight or do a drive-by on rival gang members, hoping to at least kill some rivals and make a name for the set.

They were jacked up and angry, and looking for a fight—with anyone.

The passenger is watching the cop on his side, waiting for the cop to make a mistake, look away, lose his focus just for a second.

Finally, the moment came, and the back up looked down—just for a moment. The passenger took the opportunity and pulled a gun from his waist, twisting around almost 180 degrees in the front seat and pointing the gun at the back up officer, who was still looking down.

When the back up officer looked up, he was staring at the barrel of a stolen Glock 40 caliber handgun pointed at his face. The banger pulled the trigger.

Simultaneously, the primary officer was watching, and he pulled his gun and shot. He fired three rounds into the passenger while the driver was still sitting in the car, holding the steering wheel, gunpowder burning her face and eyes; the gun was that close when the shooting started.

She screamed and exits the car, running as fast as she could, screaming the entire way.

She was later located after people called the cops to report a hysterical screaming woman in the hallway of a nearby apartment building.

She was so traumatized by the shooting, she had a breakdown and just sat in the hallway, screaming and crying that her boyfriend had been killed.

Meanwhile, the banger had pulled the trigger on his Glock, trying to kill the back up cop.

He was a recent parolee from prison and wanted to die a hero to his set, and he figured that killing a cop was as good a way to go out as any; however, Karma—or whatever power you believe in—had different ideas.

The bullet did not fire, and the cop learned a valuable lesson the hard way and was able to survive that moment.

The banger was shot several times by the primary officer and eventually removed from the vehicle. He somehow survived the shooting and ended up back in prison. His hero status was intact; his life, however, was destroyed. He was nineteen years old.

His attempt to shoot the backup officer was confirmed by the firing pin striking deep on the primer of the unspent bullet found in the chamber of the Glock.

The bored ride-along? He was watching all of this. Again, Karma is a bitch; be careful what you wish for—especially on the street.

When the shooting broke out, the bored ride-along went from entertained amusement park rider wishing he had some popcorn and a drink while waiting for the next thrill from the safety of the front seat of the patrol car, to terrified dumbass, hoping to survive the next few moments.

Survival instinct has two options for any animal in life or death situations: fight or flight. The "I am bored, I want to see some action" reality show wannabe exited the vehicle as fast as his ass could go.

No longer concerned with the thrill of watching real cops in action, writing paperwork and going to cold calls, he was on the front row of a real battle for survival—and life or death battles are wicked, fast, and brutal.

He sat, jaw dropped and eyes wide open while the ejected brass from the cops' weapons bounced off the hood of the patrol car in front of him.

He exited the vehicle and ran as fast as he could, not caring where he went or what else happened; he just knew he had to get the fuck out of there—and now.

Later, after the scene was secured and medical arrived to treat the severely wounded gang member, the cop sent out word about the missing ride-along, and units were sent out to look for him.

After about twenty minutes of searching, the now not-so-bored ride-along was found about a half-mile away, walking in circles in a parking lot, sobbing and in shock.

He kept repeating, "I just want to go home" over and over.

After going through an interview and completing a written statement for investigators, he was released. He elected never to ride-along again...imagine that.

ABOUT THE AUTHOR
ZACH FORTIER

ZACH FORTIER WAS A POLICE officer for over 30 years specializing in K-9, SWAT, gang, domestic violence, and sex crimes as an investigator. He has written three books about police work. The first book, *Curb-Chek,* is a case-by-case account of the streets as he worked them from the start of his career. The second book, *Street Creds*, details the time he spent in a gang task force and the cases that occurred. The third book, *Curbchek-Reload*, is by far the most gritty. The author is dangerously damaged, suffering from post-traumatic stress syndrome (PTSD) and the day-to-day violence of working the street. *Hero To Zero,* his fourth book, details the incredibly talented cops that he worked with but ended up going down in flames. Some ended up in prison and one on the FBI's ten most wanted list.

If you are looking for gritty, true crime stories, be sure to check out all of Zach Fortier's novels.

FORGET EVERYTHING YOU HAVE BEEN TOLD ABOUT WHO STARTED THE CRIPS AND WHY. MOST OF IT IS WRONG... VERY WRONG.

I AM RAYMOND WASHINGTON

THE AUTHORIZED BIOGRAPHY ABOUT THE ORIGINAL FOUNDER OF THE CRIPS

ZACH FORTIER WITH DERARD BARTON

CONTAINS OVER 50 PHOTGRAPHS, MANY NEVER SEEN BEFORE

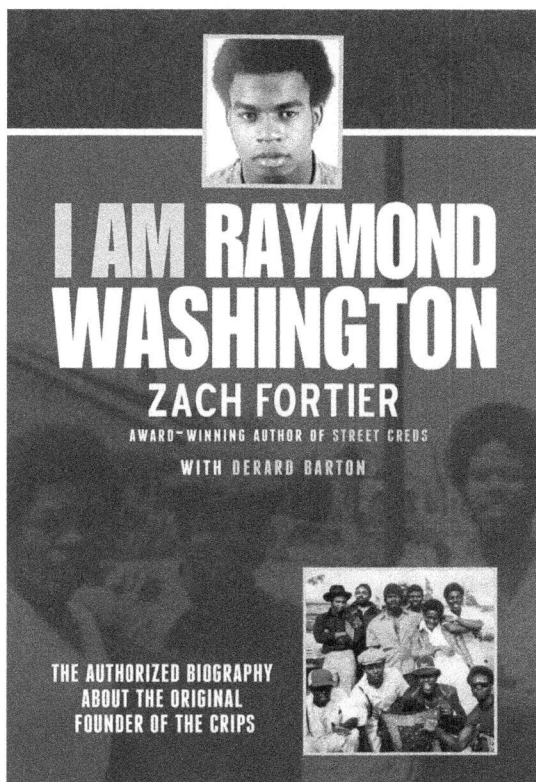

AVAILABLE IN TRADE SOFTCOVER AND EBOOK

www.ingramcontent.com/pod-product-compliance
Lightning Source LLC
Chambersburg PA
CBHW051724040426
42447CB00008B/968